The
Captured Heart

The Captured Heart

*Guarding Your Heart
in a World of Compromise*

David Holdaway

Sovereign World

Sovereign World Ltd
PO Box 777
Tonbridge
Kent TN11 0ZS
England

All Scripture quotations are taken from the New International Version unless
otherwise stated. Copyright © 1973, 1978 International Bible Society.
Published by Hodder & Stoughton

ISBN 1 85240 389 6

The publishers aim to produce books that will help to extend and build up
the Kingdom of God. We do not necessarily agree with every view expressed
by the author, or with every interpretation of Scripture expressed. We expect
each reader to make his/her judgment in the light of their own
understanding of God's Word and in an attitude of Christian love and
fellowship.

Cover design by CCD, www.ccdgroup.co.uk
Typeset by CRB Associates, Reepham, Norfolk
Printed in the United States of America

*I would like to dedicate this book to all my friends
and especially to my best friend
and loving wife Jan.*

*"Above all else, guard your heart,
for it is the wellspring of life."*
(Proverbs 4:23)

Contents

Over the Edge

'Twas a dangerous cliff as they freely confessed
Though to walk near its crest was so pleasant
But over its terrible edge there had slipped
A Duke and full many a peasant.

So the people said something would have to be done
But their project did not at all tally
Some said put a fence round the edge of the cliff
Some said "An ambulance down in the valley."

And the cry for an ambulance carried the day
For it spread to a neighbouring city
A fence may be useful or not it is true
But each heart became brim full of pity.

For those who had slipped over the terrible cliff
And the dwellers in Highway and Alley
Gave pounds and gave pence, not to put up a fence
But an ambulance down in the valley.

For the cliff is alright if you're careful they said
And if folks ever slip and are dropping
It isn't the slipping that hurts them so much
As the shock down below when they're stopping.

So day after day as the mishaps occurred
Quick forth would rescuers rally
To pick up the victims who fell down the cliff
With an ambulance down in the valley.

Better guard them when young than reclaim them when old
For the voice of true wisdom is calling
To rescue the fallen is always good, but 'tis best
To prevent them from falling.

Better close up the source of temptation and crime
Than deliver from dungeon and galley
Better build a strong fence round the top of the cliff
Than an ambulance down in the valley.

Introduction

*What captures your heart will control your life
and determine your destiny*

I was having a quiet afternoon flicking through the hundreds of channels now available on cable television and watching nothing in particular until I came across a documentary biography called *Hollywood CV*. The movie actress Cybil Shepherd was under the spotlight, which didn't interest me too much because I had never heard of her. She was it seems, incredibly beautiful in her younger days and rose to fame on Hollywood's big screen. As a young model she was spotted on the front cover of *Glamour Magazine* and cast in the starring role of the film *The Last American Picture Show*. It was at this point I came into the programme and was about to switch to yet another channel when they cut to an interview with the director of that movie. Peter Bogdonovich was at the time a thirty-one-year-old, handsome highflier in the movie industry. He said that during the production he had an affair with Shepherd, something she admitted she later regretted but he had obviously enjoyed. Then he added almost casually, "Of course his marriage and family suffered with some hearts getting broken, but we couldn't help it, we fell in love."

I shouted at the screen, "Yes you could." I knew what he was trying to say but he was wrong and so are innumerable others who use "falling in love" to justify their actions and the break up of countless marriages and families.

But how does something that can feel so right be so wrong?

"The heart is deceitful above all things" (Jeremiah 17:9). You can justify anything if you really want to and are prepared to delude yourself and excuse your sin. There are Christian leaders who have left their families to set up home with someone else and

have convinced themselves it's God's will. They commit adultery, deceive their loved ones, cheat on their spouse and say this is what God wants!

We all have the capacity to fall in love with almost anyone or anything if we open our hearts to them. When we make the choice to do this in an intimate and desirous way there comes a point when emotionally we cannot help but "fall in love". In the same way if you open a door of an areoplane at 30,000 feet and step through it you can't help but "fall". But don't blame gravity – you made the choice to open the door and step out. Adultery happens in the heart before it takes place in bed.

None of us should be complacent. Solomon warned, *"Pride goes before destruction, a haughty spirit before a fall"* (Proverbs 16:18). He also wrote, *"Above all else, guard your heart, for it is the wellspring of life"* (Proverbs 4:23), but when you read 1 Kings 11 you discover Solomon had seven hundred wives and three hundred concubines. He loved many foreign women and sought to expand the power of his empire through marital alliances, but instead of strengthening the nation he brought the judgment of God, which resulted in dividing it. Whenever we seek to build God's Kingdom by worldly methods it may have initial success but it will always end in pain and failure. Note how many times the heart is referred to in Solomon's tragic decline.

> *"King Solomon, however, loved many foreign women besides Pharaoh's daughter – Moabites, Ammonites, Edomites, Sidonians and Hittites. They were from nations about which the LORD had told the Israelites, 'You must not intermarry with them, because they will surely turn your **hearts** after their gods.' . . . As Solomon grew old, his wives turned his **heart** after other gods, and his **heart** was not fully devoted to the LORD his God, as the **heart** of David his father had been."*   (1 Kings 11:1–2, 4)

Solomon opened up his heart to that which God had said "no". But why did he also worship their gods? Because physical adultery invariably leads to spiritual adultery. The sexual act is so powerful it creates a soul tie, a bringing together not only of the body but also of the spirit. This is why Paul warns the Corinthian church so strongly about sex outside of the marriage covenant. Every night in Corinth a thousand male and female temple prostitutes invaded the streets. It was notorious for its immorality and Paul tells them there is no such thing as a one-night stand. Sexual union brings with it a human spirit to human spirit encounter. It is never just a physical or emotional act. Two become one. Sexual intercourse and intimacy is not simply the joining of two bodies, it is the union of two spirits. You will always leave something of yourself and take something of the other person after the encounter is over. You also join yourself in some measure to whatever they have given themselves. Solomon ended up sleeping with the women and worshiping their gods.

This book is not primarily about marriage and relationships it's about every issue of life. Whatever we open up our hearts to, we give the power to bless or curse us. The New Testament scholar William Barclay tells the tragic case of Robertson Nicoll, a famous editor of his day, who was born in a manse in the North East of Scotland. His father had one passion – to buy books. He was a minister and never earned more than £200 a year, but he amassed the greatest private library in Scotland amounting to 17,000 books that took over the house, the family's finances and eventually their life. He did not even use them in his sermons, he was simply consumed to own and to read them. When he was forty he married a girl of twenty-four, but in eight years his young wife was dead with tuberculosis. Of a family of five children only two lived to be over twenty. Barclay comments, "That cancerous growth of books filled every room and every passageway in the manse, it may have delighted the owner of the books, but it killed his wife and family."[1]

With most people it's not books but it may be fashion, music, a hobby, a sport, a career or a pastime. These are not wrong in themselves, except when they take the place in your heart that belongs to God and those precious to you. There are many sports fans more faithful to their club than to their wives and spend more time and money on their team than on their children. They may get divorced many times but they stay with one club for life. One famous football manager, Bill Shanklin who took Liverpool to great success in the 1970s summed it up when he said, "Some people say that football is a matter of life and death. I can tell you it is far more serious than that."

In the following chapters we are going to deal with such things as money, sex, pride, idolatry, forgiveness, righteousness, thankfulness, discouragement, betrayal and much more. The book is in two parts. The first seeks to answer the question "why" guarding our heart is so important. The second deals with the all-important issue of "how". Chapter thirteen is a practical checklist with seven tests you can take to measure who or what has captured your heart. The last chapter is about having, "A heart after God".

Gifting and anointing are vital but it is the heart that carries them. Many of you who read this book will know someone who once had a powerful ministry but has now backslidden and doesn't even attend church anymore. Charisma without character creates confusion and ultimately failure and heartache. Our gifting may get us started but it is only character that will sustain us. Integrity always has been and always will be more important than image.

PART ONE

Why Guarding Our Heart Is So Important

Chapter 1

The Primary Target

The heart of the human problem
is the problem of the human heart.

"We have all sinned," I announced to the congregation. Not much of a surprise for most as they had heard it many times and believed it fully. "We have all committed the greatest sin," I continued. This really got their attention and most weren't sure whether to say amen or scratch their heads and shout "What?" I went on to explain that all sin is a violation against the character and commandments of God. When Jesus was asked what was the greatest commandment, He replied, *"Love the Lord your God with all your heart and with all your soul and with all your mind and with all your strength"* (Mark 12:30). Therefore the greatest sin is the breaking of the greatest commandment. When we break this command we open our lives to violate every other law of God, but when we keep it we position ourselves to receive all that God desires to give us and do through us. This is why our heart is both God's and the devil's primary target. Jesus is also highlighting that what God desires more than anything else is to be loved. It is about relationship not religious observance.

According to general scriptural usage the heart is used as the most comprehensive term to describe the whole person. While it includes the affections and the emotions and even at times the mind, it is much more. It is the master control area of life. It is the fount out of which everything else comes and is why the heart is described as the source of all our troubles:

> *"The good man brings good things out of the good stored up in his heart, and the evil man brings evil things out of the evil stored up in his heart. For out of the overflow of his heart his mouth speaks."* (Luke 6:45)

"For out of the heart come evil thoughts, murder, adultery, sexual immorality, theft, false testimony, slander."

(Matthew 15:19)

The prophet Jeremiah warned, *"The heart is deceitful above all things and beyond cure"* (Jeremiah 17:9). But he also spoke of a time when God would make a New Covenant that involved the changing of the heart. In Jeremiah 31 we probably come closer to the New Testament and the Gospel than anywhere else in the Old Testament. God is going to make a New Covenant because the old one had failed and wasn't working. There was nothing wrong with the Covenant but there was something terribly wrong with the people with whom it was made. The problem was the heart. It is not insignificant that the last word in the Old Covenant is *"curse"* (Malachi 4:6).

It was Albert Einstein, the famous scientist, who said, "The real problem is in the hearts and minds of men. It is not a problem of physics but of ethics. It is easier to denature plutonium than to denature the evil spirit of man." Psalm 14:1 says, *"The fool says in his heart, 'There is no God.'"* The word "fool" is not just a reference to a person who is mentally foolish but to those who are morally flawed. The Duke of Wellington observed in his day, and how much more relevant it is to ours that "education without morality only ends up making clever devils out of people". The same week exam boards in Britain were announcing record A-level results, the newspapers were reporting an epidemic in sexually transmitted diseases and the arrest of young people abroad for indecency and obscene behavior. Some of them were students celebrating their academic success. D.L. Moody the great American Evangelist wryly commented, "If a man is stealing nuts and bolts from a railway track and, in order to change him you send him to college, at the end of his education he will steal the whole railway track."[1]

As a man thinks in his heart so is he

When I was a young Christian I heard the story of a new convert who constantly battled with temptation and became very discouraged. He finally went to see his minister and explained what was going on inside him. "It's like a war with a white dog and a black dog constantly fighting." "Which one wins?" asked his pastor. "The one I feed the most," he replied. Whatever we starve gets weaker and that which we nourish grows stronger. I never forgot the message.

Even as Christians we still have to battle with what the Bible calls the flesh. Our human spirit has been born again and is filled with the life and presence of the Holy Spirit but our flesh is full of pride and self. When we face temptation our spirit says, "honour God," but the flesh shouts "go on do it, everyone else is." Our spirit is always willing to give, serve and love but our flesh wants to get, to control, to lust. The reason sin dominates any part of a believer's life is because the flesh in that area is overcoming their spirit. Both our spirit and flesh are fed from the soul, which are the heart, the mind and the will. What goes into them will strengthen either our spirit or our flesh.

You can tell those who have lived with a heart after God for they have learned to live out of His deposit within their spirit. Even in old age when their body is frail, their will restricted and when their mind has lost its sharpness they still have peace and joy and a wonderful contentment about them. They have dug deep wells in God that they are drawing from. Those who grow old and all they have done is feed their flesh become a shadow of themselves.

I will never forget "Pop Hayes". He was the youngest ninety-year-old I have ever met. It was my joy to visit him regularly when I was an assistant minister at my first church. He had been a Christian for over sixty years and was full of the Holy Spirit. He became increasingly house bound, deaf, frail and fragile but he had a radiant spirit. He used to joke about what he called his telephone ministry. He would turn the volume up full on his specially adapted phone to call and encourage those whom God had laid on his heart. His face used to shine with a huge smile as he told me, "I have had a wonderful past but I have got an even better future."

Mind sets and belief systems

The way we think is a combination of our convictions, experiences, upbringing, environment, education, conscience, culture and belief systems. In his groundbreaking book, *Power Evangelism*, John Wimber highlights how people have learned to think differently, in his chapter on Signs and Wonders and Worldviews, he says,

"Shortly after WWII, sociologists went to the Far East to investigate Asians' attitudes and thinking processes, to see how their thinking differed from the West's. They interviewed several thousand people, receiving surprising responses to the questions on logical syllogisms – questions based on rational processes. A typical question was, 'Cotton doesn't grow in cold weather countries. England is a cold-weather country. Does cotton grow in England?' The majority of the Asians who answered the question said that they were not qualified to answer because, 'I haven't been to England.' In Western nations, most primary school children would have responded, 'No, cotton cannot grow in England. It is too cold.'. From earliest childhood Western people are trained in deductive reasoning – based on rules of logic, we draw conclusions that guide our lives. The presupposition of our culture encourages us to think this way. The assumptions of most Eastern, African, and South American cultures do not – their cultures have more of an experiential base. The exception to this is found among formally educated people. This does not mean Western culture is superior, only that it is different."[2]

Having lived in England I can tell you cotton does not grow there, but if you were to create the right atmosphere for it in a greenhouse it can grow almost anywhere.

A few years ago my wife Jan and I were in Canada, which is a beautiful and vast country. We decided one morning to visit one of the nearby shopping centers and noted on the map in our hotel room it was about five minutes away. I said to Jan, "That's not too far to walk." It was only our second time in North America and what we didn't realise is that all the distances were in the time it took to drive. Almost two hours later we finally made it to the mall tired and exhausted. When we read "five minutes", we automatically thought in terms of walking but Canadians would immediately think of "driving". We didn't see anyone else walking to the mall.

In one of the churches we pastored there was a very godly young man from Africa who had come to study at the university. After the church service one Sunday morning a couple that had recently started attending, came to see my wife – they were in fits of laughter. They were not making fun of this person but couldn't help but see the funny side of what had just happened.

They had invited him to their home for a meal and checked out if he was comfortable with dogs since they had one. He responded in total seriousness, "No, I don't eat dogs." He processed the question in a way they had not even thought of.

What we think is determined by the way we have learned to think, and the heart affects this far more than many realise. It influences our understanding of life, what we say and what we believe. Take politics for example. Two clever intellectuals who have studied all the data regarding a specific issue end up taking completely opposing views as to the best way to proceed. One is a confirmed socialist and the other a committed capitalist. I come from a town in South Wales that elected the first socialist MP to Parliament, Keir Hardy. To this day it has the largest Labour Party majority in the country. When I went to Bible College in Surrey, England, politically it was like leaving an ocean of red for a sea of blue, it could not have been more different. A common saying I heard growing up in the South Wales Valleys was, "If a donkey stood for Labour it would win," meaning the people would rather have a socialist donkey than a Tory member. In Surrey it was the other way around. I am sure they would rather have a Conservative of any kind than a Labour MP.

To help us through college my wife and I worked on a farming estate. This paid the rent for the little cottage we lived in. The lady we worked for was very kind and gracious and had a beautiful black labrador called, "Thatcher". She admired Margaret and all things blue. During the high unemployment of the early 1980s she said in all sincerity to my wife, "I really don't understand why people can't get jobs, I know many of my friends who need their lawns mowed." Where we came from most people didn't have lawns. She wasn't being pompous but simply processing the problem the only way she could.

Politicians, academics, scientists and philosophers, the list is endless, are not just the product of their intellect but even more so their hearts. One great scientist says, "I see no evidence for God and a Creator" while another like Sir Isaac Newton, arguably the greatest of them declared, "All my discoveries have been made in answer to prayer." Louis Pasteur said, "The more I study nature, the more I am amazed at the Creator." Sir James Simpson, who discovered and pioneered the use of chloroform, when asked by a student during a lecture, "What do you consider your greatest discovery?" replied, "Jesus Christ as my Saviour."[3]

Another man who has had huge influence on the twentieth century is Sigmund Freud. He has been called, "The father of modern psychology". Even though many of his ideas and theories are now discarded and discredited his legacy on our culture has been disastrous. His insistence that "Libido", the sex drive, is the prime mover, the reason that everything exists provided much of the philosophical basis for the sexual promiscuity with all its disastrous consequences in our society today.

Published in 1884, his book *Uber Coca* extolled the benefits of a white powder extracted from the coca leaf. "Exhilaration and lasting euphoria, which in no way differs from the normal euphoria of the healthy person ... You perceive an increase in self-control and possess more vitality and capacity for work. In other words you are simply more normal and it is soon hard to believe that you are under the influence of any drug." The white powder whose use he is extolling is cocaine. Let him tell that to the multitudes of lives it has demeaned and destroyed.

Freud was an atheist and though part of a Jewish family, he never formally adopted the Jewish religion. He taught that belief in God was a kind of neurosis and mental disorder.[4] He knew no theology and little about the Bible yet writes off Christianity as wish-fulfillment and obsessional neurosis. He was supremely self-confident and arrogant and accused his critics of being insane. He said of himself, "I have examined myself thoroughly and have come to the conclusion that I do not need to change much."

When you read the lives of some of those most hostile to God, you discover that before they formulated their philosophies and theories somewhere, at sometime, hurt, anger, bitterness, rejection, hatred, pain entered their heart which shaped the way they learned to think.

Lenin, the founder of modern Communism grew to hate God. At the age of sixteen he became upset by a remark of a priest he overheard talking to his father. "If your son does not go to church willingly beat him."[5] As Lenin heard it he tore off the cross he wore around his neck. The poison that entered his heart darkened his mind. His favorite philosopher, whose writings he would later widely distribute, was Holbach who had written, "God is my personal enemy." Alexander Solzhenitsyn observed, "Within the philosophical system of Marx and Lenin and at the heart of their psychology, hatred of God was the principal driving force."[6] This hostility led Lenin as the "father" of the

Russian revolution, to try and destroy the church and perfect the science of mass killings and total merciless brutality as the ultimate method of political control.

The theories of Charles Robert Darwin continue to have a huge influence in our world. Baptized as an Anglican and brought up to pray, he says that as a child he used to run the mile or so from home to school, "I often had to run very quickly to be on time, and from being a fleet runner was generally successful; but when in doubt I prayed earnestly to God to help me, and I well remember that I attributed my success to the prayers and not to my quick running, and marveled how generally I was aided."[7]

His mother died when he was only eight years of age and this seems to have had a significant influence on his later outlook in life. In 1851, his dearly loved daughter Annie, aged ten, died from what the attending physician called a "bilious fever with typhoid character". Darwin was devastated and her death seemed to hammer a final nail into his faith in God and Christian belief. In 1857 he consulted a clairvoyant and in the years that followed, attended séances and met mediums. It is said that when he visited his first clairvoyant, she shrank back in terror and exclaimed she could see within him, "A most appalling picture of horrors".[8] Just two years later on 24 November, 1859, he published *The Origin of Species* containing his theories about evolution and natural selection. He experienced considerable trauma with this. In the year leading up to publication he was rarely able to write for more than twenty minutes at a time without stomach pains, and he finished the proofs on 1 October, 1859, in between fits of vomiting. Ten days before the proofs were bound he wrote to his friend J.D. Hooker, "I have been very bad lately; having had an awful 'crisis,' one leg swelled like elephantiasis; eyes almost closed up; covered with a rash and fiery boils – but they tell me it will surely do me much good – it was like living in Hell."[9] His modern biographers talk of his self-doubt, his nagging, gnawing fear that "I have devoted my life to a fantasy."[10] He was too sick to be on hand in London when the first copies were sold. He wrote to Hooker, "I should suppose few human beings had vomited so often during the last five months."[11]

Yet strangely he remained an avid supporter of Christian missions to the day he died. During his voyage on *HMS Beagle* (1831–1836) he became an admirer of Christian missionary work. In his journal he praises the work of the missionaries in Tahiti: "The missionaries have done much in improving the Tahitian's moral character and still more in teaching them the arts of civilization."[12]

In New Zealand, he was appalled at the horrors of cannibalism and acknowledges what the Christian missionaries had done to eliminate this evil. It was the Yaghan Indians of Tierra del Fuego who most attracted Darwin's attention. When he first encountered them in December 1832, their "Savage and wild appearance and their barbarous ways made an indelible impression on him. Such was their state that he wondered if, in fact, they might be one of the missing links he was looking for." Later in correspondence with his lifelong friend, Rear Admiral Sir James Sullivan, he reveals his great surprise and incredulity at the changes taking place amongst the Tierra del Fuego Indians as a result of the missionary efforts to evangelise and educate them. Such was his admiration for the work that he became a supporter of the South American Missionary Society during the last fifteen years of his life. He even asked if the Mission's committee might elect him as an honorary member of the Society. He said that it would make him so proud to be part of such a great work.[13]

Sir James later recalled that not many weeks before Darwin's death, Darwin had sent him the annual subscription to the South American Missionary Society with the comment: "Judging from the missionary journal the mission on Tierra del Fuego seems to be going on quite wonderfully well."[14]

The theory of evolution is embraced by multitudes today not because it is proven or provable, but because the alternative of a Creator to whom we will give an account for the way we live, is unthinkable. Physicist and writer Paul Davies expresses this in an article in *National Geographic*:

> "Even on earth the origin of life is a stubbornly enduring mystery. How can a collection of chemicals form themselves into a living thing without any interference from outside? On the face of it life is an exceedingly unlikely event. There is no known principle that matter says it has to organise itself into life. I'm very happy to believe in my head that we live in a biofriendly universe, because in my heart I find it very congenial."[15]

In spite of the cherished idea most people have that they make decisions on the basis of logical reasoning, every salesman and advertising executive knows that to bring people to a point of decision they have to move the emotions and feelings. Generally the rational faculties are used afterwards to find reasons to justify the decisions made.

Almost every month some bank or loan company sends me a letter with a specimen cheque asking that I imagine what I could do with it. They include a picture of a new car, a holiday, and luxury conservatory. They don't want me to think but first of all imagine. They are appealing to my heart rather than my head. They are selling a dream not a debt. Then they tell me I can have it all at a special interest rate and the offer is really too good to miss. Only now are they addressing my reasoning by telling me why I should justify my heart's desire. The result is we end up getting things we don't need to impress people we don't like with finance we can't afford!

Many who believe they are thinking through the issues are in reality merely rearranging their prejudices. Two sets of rival football fans can see a foul and come to totally opposite views of what took place. One is convinced it's a dive and the other adamant that it's a penalty. Both claim to be making an educated reponse.

Just imagine with me for a moment, two men looking out over the poverty-stricken communities in the Third World. The children are vulnerable and defenceless; the parents are down-trodden and downcast. Both these men see exactly the same conditions but they think totally differently. One whose lifestyle is perverted and corrupt sees an opportunity to satisfy his lusts. (He sees a haven of sexual perversion to exploit child prostitution.) The other whose character is altogether different says, "Something has to be done to help and protect these children" and starts thinking of ways in which to do it. This is not simply an emotional reaction but a reasoned response.

When we are told that what matters in public life is a person's abilities and talents and not their ethics or morality don't you believe it. If someone can't be trusted to be loyal to his wife and children what makes you think he will be loyal to anyone or anything else? The person who cheats on those closest to them has learned to think a certain way and will cheat on anyone else when it suits them. The values we hold in our heart determine the morals we display in our lives, the conclusions we come to and the decisions we make.

Chapter 2

Money, Pride and Sex

*You never really know what is in your heart
until it is tried, tested or tempted.*

Charisma is one of America's leading Christian magazines. It stated in its January 2002 editorial why it was no longer going to focus on big name ministers and ministries on its cover pages:

> "This magazine has had its share of Christian celebrities on its covers: Pastors of megachurches, award-winning musicians, best-selling authors, you name it. We all love famous people perhaps because we envy their success or maybe because we are just curious whether they have flaws. In the end, these flawed celebrities often disappoint us. Ten of the ministry leaders we featured on the covers of *Charisma* in the 1980s eventually endured embarrassing scandals. And two of the six megachurches we featured 16 years ago in a series called 'Outstanding Churches of America' disbanded because of moral failures.
>
> As much as we hate to admit it, bigger is not necessarily better, and the applause of men rarely has anything to do with God's favour. What seems to glitter with success today may not stand the heat of God's refining fire tomorrow. What grabs the spotlight usually turns out to be a distracting sideshow. We have decided to focus more of our coverage on unsung heroes – the average folks who are happy to serve Jesus whether or not anyone applauds their sacrifice or writes about them in a magazine."

The cult of image and self-promotion has probably never been greater or more dangerous both inside and outside the church. There is often more hype than hope and style is exalted over substance. Elijah knew that the real fire of God falls from above and his command to *"Put no fire under the altar"* is both a warning and wake up call for us all today. There are enough counterfeits in the world. The last thing we need in the church is false, man-made fire. We may become experts in our presentation but unless we keep our hearts right before God we will inevitably discover that the "wages of spin is death".

Billy Graham, who has lived and ministered with great integrity in our generation, said the three greatest temptations he encountered in his life and ministry were money, pride and sex. They have been called, "The Big Three".

Money

A.W. Tozer wryly observed, "Christians don't tell lies, they sing them in their hymns."[1] We sing about our willingness to give and surrender until the offering basket comes or we are chal-lenged to go outside our comfort zones. It reminds me of the occasion when the huge brass collection plates were passed around the church and returned almost empty to the vicar. He took them, held them up to heaven and prayed, "Lord, we thank you for the safe return of these plates."

Tozer goes on to say in his book *I Talk Back to the Devil*, "Money often comes between men and God. Someone has said that you can take two small ten-cent pieces and shut out the view of a panoramic landscape. Go to the mountains and just hold two coins closely in front of your eyes – the mountains are still there, but you cannot see them at all because there is a coin shutting off the vision in each eye."

It doesn't take a lot of money – just a little, positioned in the wrong place – to effectively obscure our vision of God. Such is its power that many who trust God for eternal life in heaven don't trust Him with their finances here on earth. The devil hides behind this power of money because he knows that true followers of Jesus will not bow to him, but if he can get them to bow down to money he will use it to pull their strings. They become the puppets and he their puppet master. This is why Jesus said,

> *"No-one can serve two masters. Either he will hate the one and love the other, or he will be devoted to the one and despise the other. You cannot serve both God and Money."* (Matthew 6:24)

The first sin the Holy Spirit records of the Israelites in the Promised Land had to do with the lure of riches. Achan brought defeat on the nation and the judgment of God on himself and his family (Joshua 7:24). The first sin the Holy Spirit records for us in the Early Church is again associated with deceit and money:

> *"Then Peter said, 'Ananias, how is it that Satan has so filled your heart that you have lied to the Holy Spirit and have kept for yourself some of the money you received for the land? ... You have not lied to men but to God.' When Ananias heard this, he fell down and died ... "* (Acts 5:3, 4–5)

That must have been a terrifyingly dramatic moment and more was to follow when Ananias's wife Sapphira came in later and lied and also died. Note Peter's words to Ananias, *"Satan has so filled your heart."*

The great revivalist and founder of Methodism, John Wesley, warned frequently about the dangers of money. He knew well its power over his own life, which led him to say, "When I have any money I get rid of it as quickly as possible, lest it find a way into my heart."

A golden calf or a tabernacle?

When Moses led the Israelites out of Egypt, God saw to it that four hundred years of labor didn't go without payment, they were loaded down with the treasures of Egypt. But what good was gold in the desert? It was to be for both a test and a testimony. There are two significant accounts of what they did with their wealth that teach us a great deal. When Moses was on the mountain with God the people rebelled. They took their treasure and threw it into a furnace and made a calf of gold, engaging in idolatry, which brought the judgment of God (Exodus 32).

At the same time that God was giving instructions to Moses about building a tabernacle, the devil was inciting the people to use their riches to make an idol. Satan uses the love of money not only to trap people in its pursuit but also to hinder the purposes of God's work.

Later Moses called for the people to give to the building of the tabernacle and they brought so much that he had to tell them to stop. (What a problem to have!) They came with gold, silver, bronze, fine cloth, animal skins, fragrances and incense to make

a dwelling where God would come in His glory (Exodus 35:5 –
36:7).

You can either take the blessing that God gives you, your
treasures and talents, and build a golden calf and fall down and
worship it, or you can bring them to God and let Him make a
tabernacle where He dwells and reveals His glory. Money can
either become an idol we serve or, like Wesley and countless
others, an instrument which we use to worship God.

What we do with our money is about far more than our attitude
to giving. It is the visible expression of our life. We go to work and
in return for our time and ability we receive money. Therefore,
when we give we are not simply putting notes and coins into the
offering but that which represents our life. The principle of
the tithe is that we recognise God is to be first and foremost.

> *"Honour the* LORD *with your wealth,*
>   *with the firstfruits of all your crops;*
> *then your barns will be filled to overflowing,*
>   *and your vats will brim over with new wine."*
>
> (Proverbs 3:9–10)

If we eat our financial seed instead of sowing it we may know
some immediate pleasure and provision but we will never
experience the harvest of God's abundant fullness. Like Esau we
sacrifice our birthright for a bowl of stew.

Do you have money or does money have you? Do you own
possessions or do possessions possess you? There is nothing wrong in having riches, the problem comes when they
have captured your heart. But how do you know when you have
crossed the line?

1. Anything you can't give away that God tells you to give
   means that you don't have it – it has you.

2. Whenever possessions have become more valued than
   people, or riches more important than relationships you
   have crossed the line.

3. When you can't stop wanting or worrying about possessions, they have captured your heart. There is nothing
   wrong in having nice things but Jesus said, *"the pagans run
   after all these things"* (Matthew 6:32). It is their passion and
   pursuit that has captured them.

Frank Sinatra's daughter, Tina, published a book a few years ago about her famous father, *My Father's Daughter*. She says that towards the end of his life:

> "His health was in tatters and he had become mired in financial wrangles, but my father refused to stop giving concerts. 'I've just got to earn more money,' he would say. His performances, sad to say, were becoming more and more uneven. Uncertain of his memory he became dependent on tele prompters. When I saw him at the *Desert Inn* in Las Vegas he struggled through the show and felt so sickly at the end that he needed oxygen from a tank that he kept on hand. At another show he forgot the lyrics to the song, 'Second Time Around', a ballad he had sung a thousand times and his adoring audience finished it for him. I couldn't bear to see dad struggle.
>
> I remembered all the times he repeated the old boxing maxim, 'You gotta get out before you hit the mat'. He wanted to retire at the top of his game and I always thought he would know when his time came but pushing 80 he lost track of when to quit. After seeing one too many of these fiasco's I told him, 'Pop, you can stop now you don't have to stay on the road.' With a stricken expression he said, 'No, I've got to earn more money, I have to make sure everyone is taken care of.'"[2]

When I read that I understood why he had so many "come backs" after retiring. The tragedy is that he was already worth a fortune and after his death his family were torn apart over the money he left.

Pride

This was the first sin and it happened within the heart. Lucifer, the archangel who led the worship of God in heaven, was a creation of incredible beauty and splendor. He is described in Ezekiel as the "anointed cherub" and in Isaiah as the *"morning star"*, the *"son of the dawn"*. But his heart became filled with his own importance and he envied the place of God. Pride and the lust for power and position captured his heart and ever since he has targeted the heart in the same way.

"Your heart became proud
   on account of your beauty,
and you corrupted your wisdom
   because of your splendour.
So I threw you to the earth;
   I made a spectacle of you before kings."   (Ezekiel 28:17)

"You said in your heart,
   'I will ascend to heaven;
I will raise my throne
   above the stars of God;
I will sit enthroned on the mount of assembly,
   on the utmost heights of the sacred mountain.
I will ascend above the tops of the clouds;
   I will make myself like the Most High.'
But you are brought down to the grave,
   to the depths of the pit."   (Isaiah 14:13–15)

When God is looking to raise someone up it's not their academic CV or human references and life's accomplishments he looks at, but their heart. When the disciples were choosing a successor for Judas they prayed as to whether it should be Joseph or Matthias, *"Lord, you know everyone's heart. Show us, which of these two you have chosen"* (Acts 1:24). We are not to make leaders in God's Kingdom but we are to recognise as leaders those God has chosen. For someone to be appointed whom God has not anointed is a tragedy not only for them but those who elected them. Dr Martyn Lloyd-Jones used to say, "The worst thing that can happen to a man is to be promoted before he is ready."

In his book, *Compassion and Self-Hate* Theodore Isaac Rubin describes his own struggles with pride in his desire to become a great lecturer who wowed people and the terrible toll it took on him. At the end of his lectures he knew only headaches and intense ego aches. Seeking to understand himself and what was happening, he distinguished between those who participate and those who have to perform. Participants are fully involved in their presentations. They throw themselves into their topic yet they are themselves as they speak. They allow their limitations to show and do not recriminate themselves for doing so. While performers aren't necessarily exhibitionists, they do speak in a way that does not fully fit their personalities. They are driven by a need to perform because they are self-conscious, afraid of derision by others and are trying to hide their limitations. They live in a fear of failure and rejection.

Before accepting his limitations Rubin expected to give a brilliant performance of himself every time he lectured. Each time had to be better than the last. "I was split three ways. One of me was lecturing, one of me was watching me and one of me was watching the audience." He says that self-hate lurked if he failed and he couldn't give himself single-mindedly to his lecture under such severe self-surveillance. He almost gave up lecturing all together because of the high cost it was exacting. Finally he asked himself, "Do I expect to leave listeners ecstatic over my impassioned artful rendition? Do I want to be a performer?" When he could finally answer no to both questions he was free to give lectures that helped rather than just impressed people.

The writer and theologian J.B. Phillips was another who suffered and struggled with these same issues. He was a brilliant academic and his translation of the Gospels and New Testament into modern English along with his countless best-selling books, radio and teaching ministry made him a household name in Christian circles. Yet he suffered terribly with depression and feelings of inadequacy and self-doubt. His close friend, Edwin Robertson, drawing extensively on biographical materials and letters as well as conversations with Phillip's wife, Vera, tells of a brilliant man tormented across fifty years of ministry by his slavery to perfectionism. He says that Phillips' tremendous need to excel through preaching, radio broadcasts and writing drove him to exclaim, "I would rather die than be ordinary" and "I just can't bear anyone to criticise me or see me fail." Yet when success did come it was so dreary and pointless that at the time this famous translator and Bible scholar enjoyed fame he was in the care of a succession of psychiatrists and counselors.

Roy Cripps writing in the Christian magazine *Guideposts*, told about a visit made to Phillips' home in Swansea just after Phillips emerged from this dark and protracted period of his life. He was told by Phillips: "Satan was mounting his most devastating attack on me. He was building an image of J.B. Phillips that was not J.B. Phillips at all. I was no longer an ordinary human being. I was in danger of becoming a super Christian. Everything I wrote had to be better than the last and the image grew until it was so unlike me that I could no longer live with it and yet the thought of destroying it was terrifying too. It was on this dilemma I was hung." He went on to tell Cripps how he had been powerfully influenced by a vision of C.S. Lewis just a few days after Lewis died. In the vision Lewis said to Phillips, "It's not as hard as you think, you know." Phillips then related to Cripps his own conclusion to his crisis, "It's a glorious thing to be yourself."[3]

None of us are God's adults or scholars; we are and always will be children. No one comes to Him as a professor or minister, banker, doctor, chairman of the company, queen or king. We can only ever come as a sinner seeking forgiveness or as a child to their Heavenly Father. None of our titles impress Him. The late professor James Denney, of Scotland, warned every Christian and especially preachers, "No man can bear witness to Christ and to himself at the same time. No man can give the impression that he himself is clever and that Christ is mighty to save."[4]

Someone once asked Corrie ten Boom if she had a hard time staying humble. She told him, "When Jesus rode into Jerusalem on Palm Sunday on the back of a donkey, and everyone was waving palm branches and throwing garments on the road and singing praises, do you think that for one moment it even entered the head of that donkey that any of it was for him?" She smiled and went on, "If I can be the donkey on which Jesus Christ rides in His glory, I give Him all the praise and all the honour."

When Lucifer's heart was filled with pride and lust for power a doomsday virus was unleashed into the universe. But God provided an antidote. Jesus, who is God, was willing to humble Himself and become obedient unto death. The devil was cast down to the lowest place and Jesus exalted to the highest.

> *"For whoever exalts himself will be humbled, and whoever humbles himself will be exalted."*   (Matthew 23:12)

This is a good place to stop and search our own heart.

We will talk about sex in the next chapter.

Chapter 3

Sex

A sweet flirtation not quite adultery but adulteration.
(Lord Byron)

We are going to get very serious in a few moments because sex is such a sacred gift. Sadly, it is also something that has given itself to extremes. Some people never stop talking about it while for others it is an unmentionable subject, especially in church. Let me try and break the ice by telling you a story about a minister who was in despair at the failure of his sermons. Somehow, he never chose a subject that grabbed the attention of the congregation, something that made them sit up, think, change their lives – or at least come up to him afterwards, shake his hand and say, "Thank you, what a helpful sermon." No, unfortunately those who did not fall asleep during his sermons, sneaked past him at the porch or gave a limp handshake and a formal, "Good morning, reverend." Things came to a head one weekend when trying to prepare his sermon, he stormed out of his study and said to his wife, "What's the use? I might as well climb into the pulpit and talk about riding bicycles."

"Don't be absurd," said his wife. "Well, why not – it would shake them out of their complacency – a totally unexpected, unusual subject – you never know." So "Riding Bicycles" it was. His wife was very apprehensive, but she went into the crèche, as she did every morning service, leaving her husband to face the congregation alone. But as he climbed the pulpit steps, unknown to her, a far more brilliant idea entered his head. "Not 'riding bicycles' no, that'll never wake them up," he thought, "I'll preach on sex. I'll startle the whole congregation and preach a frank, searching, compelling sermon – on **sex**!"

And he did. And it was brilliant. It was funny. It was honest. It was moving. It came from the heart. It was the sermon of his life. Afterwards, the congregation mobbed him. They came up to him, shook his hand, thanked him for taking the lid off so many problems, for his sympathetic insight. A woman rushed into the crèche and went up to the minister's wife. "Your husband was wonderful!" she said. "You should have heard his sermon. Such a brilliant choice of subject." "Really?" said his wife, astonished. "I thought it was a very odd choice considering he's only done it three times in his life. To be perfectly honest with you," she whispered confidentially, "the first time he fell over and the second time his hat blew off."

A theology professor asked his class on homiletics (the study of preaching), "How often do you think about prophecy?" One student answered, "Several times a year." "And how often do you have sexual thoughts?" The young man replied, "Several times a day." This is why the Bible has a great deal to say about sex. The first command God ever gave was a sexual command, *"Be fruitful and multiply."*

Sex is not a four-letter word. It is a beautiful gift from God to be enjoyed within the covenant of marriage. It is His creation not the devil's so let's nail the lie that the devil is for it and God is against it. Rather God is for sex and the devil does all he can to warp, twist and corrupt it. Our bodies are made to experience exquisite pleasures and delights. Pleasure is God's invention not the devil's. Yet modern society, like the ancient world, has made a goddess of sensuality worshiping pleasure instead of receiving it with thanksgiving and as a result, men and women become slaves of their lust.

In his book *Mere Christianity* C.S. Lewis asks us to imagine that we took a trip to another country. We would be eager to learn all we possibly could about its inhabitants. One day we spot a group of people lined up in front of a theatre waiting to purchase tickets. Curious about what is going on we join them and are soon seated inside. As the show begins there is a musical fanfare. Then as the curtain slowly rises, there on the center of the stage appears, without a thing on, a lamb chop. We are startled as the audience stomps and cheers and whistles. We leave quickly and drive down the highway. We notice billboards advertising soft drinks, television sets, refrigerators and cars. But in the center of each one, no matter what the subject, you see a lamb chop. Before long we would be convinced that something had gone wrong. A perfectly legitimate pleasure like eating lamb chops had been carried to ridiculous excess. Lewis adds, "But wouldn't someone who visited earth from a distant planet think that's what happened to us regarding sex?"

It has been estimated that by the time a young person reaches eighteen they will have seen some 9,000 suggested or actual acts of intercourse portrayed by the media. The sexual drive is one of the most powerful highly-charged explosive energies a person possesses. We need to understand this God-given gift and submit it to the Lordship of Jesus.

The holiness of sex

Sex has the power to create and to destroy. The devil hates this because we have a creative capacity, something he did not possess even before he was cast out of heaven. It is a gift and profound blessing from a God of love. Yet if we step outside His order it has the capacity to degrade and demean.

In the Bible the male and female organs are held to be sacred and sexual union should be a holy encounter. The female organ in Hebrew is *Boshet*, which means "shame" in that it is shameful to speak or refer to it in a degrading manner. The male organ was circumcised as the sign of the covenant.

Hebrews 13:4 commands us to "keep the marriage bed holy". Sex can be so holy that not even the angels are allowed to look on. But when sexual activity is engaged in outside God's command and covering, it becomes a peep show for every demon and demonic power around. The devil is not all-knowing or present everywhere at the same time so how does he throw guilt, accusation and condemnation at people for sexual sin? Because his minions were there and they report back.

C.S. Lewis writing in the *Screwtape Letters* describes a senior demon giving advice to a junior on how to get people to sin. He says, "Our master will use wrong sexual relationships, he hates the momentary pleasure it brings but is willing for that because he is sure to see great pain that comes after it." Free sex is a lie. There is always a price to be paid.

Oscar Wilde had a brilliant mind and won the highest academic honours. He was a renowned writer and a man of great charm with kindly instincts but was imprisoned for his sexual activity. Listen to what he says about himself in his book *De Profundis*:

> "The gods had given me almost everything. But I let myself be lured into long spells of senseless and sensual ease ... tired of being on the heights I deliberately went to the

depths in search for new sensation. What the paradox was to me in the sphere of thought, perversity became to me in the sphere of passion. I grew careless of the lives of others. I took pleasure where it pleased me, and passed on. I forgot that every little action of the common day makes or unmakes character, and that therefore what one has done in the secret chamber, one has some day to cry aloud from the house-top. I ceased to be lord over myself. I was no longer the captain of my soul, and did not know it. I allowed pleasure to dominate me. I ended in horrible disgrace."[1]

Another who championed the cause of sexual liberation echoed Wilde's sad words. He too became enslaved by his "freedom". This is how one of the national newspapers described his life days after his pitiful death:

"Quentin Crisp was one of this century's most flamboyant homosexuals. Yesterday (Nov 21 1999) Crisp was found unconscious in a house in Chorlton, a suburb of Manchester. He was taken to hospital and pronounced dead, apparently of natural causes. Having spent the last two decades living in exile in downtown Manhattan, Crisp had only returned to England to briefly tour his latest one-man show. This was to have opened in Manchester the next day.

At the end Crisp had many friends and admirers, even receiving a card from former U.S. President Bill Clinton when he turned 90 on Christmas day 1998. But the fact that he died alone reflected the bitter unhappiness of most of his life. Unlike gay rights campaigners of today, Crisp always stated that being homosexual was a 'miserable existence', 'I didn't like it and I didn't want it' and he would not wish it on anyone.

Born Denis Pratt, he was brought up in Sutton, South London, and the youngest of four children. Crisp believed homosexuality was imparted in the genes. At 14 he went to public school. Public School was like going to jail he said later, and as in jail it is not the warders you're frightened of but the other inmates. Like many of his associates he inhabited the twilight world of prostitution. He found the sex disgusting. What he really wanted was to be loved. Eventually he came to regard love or any strong emotion as unpleasant if not impossible."[2]

The Christian psychiatrist and author John White expresses great compassion for those fallen in sexual sin and bound by its power. He says in his book, *Eros Defiled*:

> "My real concern is the loneliness, the misery and the heartaches which so often accompany sexual sin. Sex within marriage was given that human loneliness might end, reproduction was secondary with it being fitting that new life should arise out of love. It is then a paradox that what God gave to end human aloneness proves often to cause the very thing it was ordained to abolish, which is alienation. I have no heart to denounce sexual sin I am too moved by its misery. Yet I use the word sin deliberately, there are certain forms of sexual behaviour that are sinful."

One of America's greatest sports stars was the late Wilt Chamberlain. He was a prolific scorer as an NSA basketball player, but the number he will probably be remembered for most is 20,000. That is the number of women the never-married Chamberlain claimed in his autobiography to have slept with. What few may remember though, says columnist Clarence Page, is Chamberlain went on to write that he would have traded all 20,000 for the one woman he wanted to stay with for keeps.[3]

Tasmin Day-Lewis produced a Channel Four documentary series on adultery several years ago. She investigated thoroughly and concluded, "I haven't been able to find a happy adulterer."

Sex is not love

The expression "making love" is not found in the Bible because sex does not make love but rather it is love that makes sex what God intended it to be. Love is about giving and sex without this becomes lust, the desire to get, use and discard when no longer needed. Love keeps together but lust drives apart because at its heart is sin and self.

Paul's words to Timothy are filled with encouragement and warnings. He addresses specifically the issues of money, pride and sex by telling him to *"Flee the evil desires of youth, and pursue righteousness, faith, love and peace, along with those who call on the Lord out of a pure heart"* (2 Timothy 2:22). Fleeing from temptation is not running away from the devil but running to God.

When Paul wrote these words Timothy was about forty years

of age. Sexual temptation is not just a young person's problem. It is the over thirties that keep the pornography industry in business. The late Bishop Fulton Sheen once received a letter from a young man who was struggling with sexual temptation and was asked, "When will this end?" He wrote back, "Don't ask me I'm just turning 80."

Whatever our age or position we need to guard our hearts from sexual sin and its lure. Jesus spoke of it in the Sermon on the Mount saying it was a heart issue:

> *"You have heard that it was said, 'Do not commit adultery.' But I tell you that anyone who looks at a woman lustfully has already committed adultery with her in his heart."* (Matthew 5:27–28)

The book of Proverbs is all about life and wisdom and it's no coincidence that the heart is what it refers to most; sixty-nine times the heart is mentioned. Solomon warns against sexual sin and the allure of the immoral woman lest they capture our heart.

> *"Do not lust in your **heart** after her beauty*
> *or let her captivate you with her eyes."*   (Proverbs 6:25)

> *"Keep my commands and you will live;*
> *guard my teachings as the apple of your eye.*
> *Bind them on your fingers;*
> *write them on the tablet of your **heart**."*   (Proverbs 7:2–3)

> *"Do not let your **heart** turn to her ways*
> *or stray into her paths.*
> *Many are the victims she has brought down;*
> *her slain are a mighty throng.*
> *Her house is a highway to the grave,*
> *leading down to the chambers of death."* (Proverbs 7:25–27)

Thank God there is a way back for the fallen and the broken by sexual sin. The first person to see Jesus after His resurrection was a former demonised prostitute Mary Magdalene who had been set free and forgiven.

In Psalm 51 David cries out to God for mercy as he laments over his adultery and murder. As he is broken before God so is the guilt, shame and bondage that have taken him captive. In his lament he cries, *"Create in me a pure heart, O God, and renew a steadfast spirit within me"* (Psalm 51:10). David was forgiven and restored by God but sin, especially sexual sin, has social as well as spiritual consequences. What later happened among some of David's own children and their sexual iniquity ached his heart immensely.

When Jesus told the woman at the well in Samaria (John 4) to *"Go, call your husband"* He knew the man she was living with was not her husband and she had already had five husbands before him. He was saying to her that she had gone from one man to another looking for love and fulfillment but all her relationships and one-night stands had left her lonely and empty. Jesus offers her the living water of God's love and life that satisfies our greatest and deepest longing. He is also showing her that God knows everything she has ever done and still He loves her. He knows her better than anyone ever would and loves her more than anyone ever could. That is true of you and me as well.

Prayer for forgiveness and cleansing from sexual sins
Father, I confess that I have failed to resist the continuing attacks of the enemy. I confess . . . [specify]. I now agree with Your verdict on my sins. I renounce all pleasures associated with these sins. I ask You to forgive me, cleanse my memories and heal the hurts.

Lord Jesus, thank You that You died for me and paid the penalty for my sins. I acknowledge my need of You and accept You as my Savior. I invite You now to be Lord of my life – Lord of my body and all my behavior – Lord of my mind and all my thoughts – Lord of my emotions and all my reactions – Lord of my will and all my decisions – Lord of my spirit and my relationship with You. I invite You to be Lord of my sexuality, my time, my home, my family, my possessions (my marriage) and all my relationships. Thank You Jesus that Your blood was shed that I might be set free and live in freedom. Amen.

Chapter 4

Idols in the Heart

Those who cling to worthless idols
forfeit the grace that could be theirs.
(Jonah 2:8)

In his classic book *The Wounded Healer*, Henri Nouwen retells a tale from ancient India about four royal brothers who each decided to master a special ability. Time passed and the brothers met to reveal what they had learned. "I have mastered a science," said the first, "by which I can take a bone of some creature and create the flesh that goes with it." "I," said the second, "know how to grow that creature's skin and hair if there is flesh on its bones." The third said, "I am able to create its limbs." "And I," concluded the fourth, "know how to give life to that creature."

The brothers then went into the jungle to find a bone so they could demonstrate their specialties. As fate would have it, the bone they found was a lion's. One added flesh to the bone, the second grew hide and hair, the third completed it with matching limbs, and the fourth gave the lion life. Shaking its mane, the ferocious beast arose and jumped on his creators. He killed them all and vanished contentedly into the jungle.

We too have the capacity to create what can devour us. Possessions and property can turn and destroy us and goals and dreams can consume us unless we first seek God's kingdom and righteousness. Vision and hope are indispensable to a fulfilled life but even they can turn against us.

> *"Hope deferred makes the heart sick,*
> *but a longing fulfilled is a tree of life."*   (Proverbs 13:12)

We have to guard our hearts against hopes and desires that are not from God. One of the devil's wiles is to get us to dream our plans instead of God's purposes so we become frustrated and discouraged when they are unfulfilled. It's great to dream big dreams but make sure God is in them, otherwise disappointment and disillusionment may devour you. Loss of expectation will consume you. I have always found it significant that on the Day of Pentecost Peter, quoting the prophet Joel, doesn't say that old men will have dreams but they will *"dream dreams"*. They first receive the dream from God and then they dream it.

Someone might ask, "But doesn't the Bible say that God will give us the desires of our heart?" Yes it does but read the whole verse:

> *"Delight yourself in the* LORD
> *and he will give you the desires of your heart."*   (Psalm 37:4)

Our desires must be born out of loving God and putting Him first, otherwise we may be creating our own idol whether it is a ministry or a mansion, a big church or a big bank account.

Johann Sebastian Bach was one of the greatest composers of all time, yet his gift of music never became an idol to him. He said, "All music should have no other end and aim than the glory of God and the soul's refreshment."[3] He headed his compositions: "J.J." – *Jesus Juva* – which means "Jesus help me". He ended them, "S.D.G." – *Soli Dei gratia* – which means "To God alone the praise".

What is an idol?

First the longer and more technical definition:

▶ *"An idol is something whether material or mental, a carving of our hands or concept in our heads which grows larger in our heart and God smaller so eventually it becomes bigger than God."*

Now the condensed version:

▶ *"An idol is anything we put before or beside God."*

Here's the simplified meaning:

▶ *"An idol is anything that takes the place of God."*

The first two commandments God gave to Moses were that there must be no images or gods above or alongside Him. Yet even as He was saying this to Moses on Mount Sinai, the Israelites in the camp below were busy making a golden calf like the idols of Egypt to bow down and worship. Human depravity and God's judgment were the result of their sin and so began the long battle for the hearts of God's people and the sin of idolatry.

Throughout the rest of the Old Testament idolatry is the sin that God condemns more often than any other. The prophets made it clear that the actual images were lifeless carvings but operating through them were demonic forces. This is part of the deception that idolatry brings. We think we have control over what we have made, but in reality we discover like the four brothers that there are dark powers we unleash that end up ruling over us.

> *"They worshipped their idols,*
>   *which became a snare to them.*
> *They sacrificed their sons*
>   *and their daughters to demons.*
> *They shed innocent blood,*
>   *the blood of their sons and daughters,*
> *whom they sacrificed to the idols of Canaan,*
>   *and the land was desecrated by their blood.*
> *They defiled themselves by what they did;*
>   *by their deeds they prostituted themselves."*
>
> (Psalm 106:36–39)

In the New Testament Paul warns the church at Corinth that demons work through idols and images. When you bow before them you are surrendering yourself to the evil powers behind them:

> *"Consider the people of Israel: Do not those who eat the sacrifices participate in the altar? Do I mean then that a sacrifice offered to an idol is anything, or that an idol is anything? No, but the sacrifices of pagans are offered to demons, not to God, and I do not want you to be participants with demons. You cannot drink the cup of the Lord and the cup of demons too; you cannot have a part in both the Lord's table and the table of demons."*
>
> (1 Corinthians 10:18–21)

God is not only to be worshiped as the Supreme One, He is to be the Only One. Painfully, the history of the Old Testament is littered with the worship of images and idols by His people. The devil's most cunning schemes were not getting Israel to abandon and deny their God. This he knew he could never successfully do for any length of time. Their history and life was too full of God's presence and activity. Rather he seduced the people by getting them to acknowledge others' gods and place them alongside creating a syncretistic religion, a mixture of deities polluting the people's hearts. The prophets called it "spiritual adultery". The idol shrines became centers of gross sexual and demonic depravity and as we have just read even human sacrifice. God hates this mixture and what it inevitably leads to. He gave numerous laws and regulations that warned about it. Some may seem strange to us until we understand that at the heart of all God's laws is the command to, *"Be holy because I, the* LORD *your God, am holy"* (Leviticus 19:2). There was to be no mixture of seeds to be planted together in the same field. No mixture of materials used in clothing. No mating of different kinds of animals (Leviticus 19:19). It is only the pure (without mixture) in heart who will see God (Matthew 5:8).

Syncretism not atheism has always been the devil's most potent weapon. This is why so many people claim to be Christian but don't live a Christian life. They acknowledge God but bow before other gods. These idols may not be wooden carvings but rather possessions, pursuits and pleasures. The sports idol. The pop idol. The film idol. The fashion idol. The idol of self-determination that says no God in heaven is going to rule my life, "I will do it my way."

The Christians in the Early Church were persecuted and martyred not only for worshiping Jesus but because they would not worship anyone else. They were slaughtered in the Roman arenas because they refused to worship Caesar as a god alongside Jesus.

Foxe's Book of Martyrs records the harrowing details of what many of those first believers suffered,

> "The barbarities inflicted on the Christians, during the first persecution, were such as excited the sympathy of even Romans themselves. Nero nicely refined upon cruelty, and contrived all manner of punishments for his victims. He had some sewed up in the skins of wild beasts, and then attacked

by dogs till they expired; and others dressed in shirts made
stiff with wax, fixed to axle trees and set on fire in his
garden."[1]

Polycarp was one of the most famous martyrs. He was Bishop
of Smyrna, one of the seven churches mentioned in the book of
Revelation and was martyred on Saturday, 23 February, AD 155.
It was the time of the public games and the city was crowded.
The mob dragged him to the tribunal of the Roman magistrate
where he was given the inevitable choice – sacrifice to the
godhead of Caesar or die? He gave one of the most famous
replies in church history, "Eighty and six years have I served Him
and He has done me no wrong. How can I blaspheme my King
who saved me?" They took him to be burned at the stake and he
prayed his last prayer, "O Lord God Almighty, the Father of thy
well-beloved and ever blessed son, by whom we have received
the knowledge of Thee . . . I thank Thee that Thou hast graciously
thought me worthy of this day and this hour."[2] God had
captured his heart and he could bow to no other.

Idols in the heart

Before an idol is carved with the hands it is created within the
heart.

> *"I know all about Ephraim;*
>   *Israel is not hidden from me.*
> *Ephraim, you have now turned to prostitution;*
>   *Israel is corrupt.*
> *Their deeds do not permit them*
>   *to return to their God.*
> *A spirit of prostitution is in their heart;*
>   *they do not acknowledge the LORD."*   (Hosea 5:3–4)

There is a fascinating passage in the book of Ezekiel that says
that anyone who sets up idols in their hearts and seeks to know
God's will, will be answered in keeping with their great idolatry.
God does this to reveal their true condition for them to renounce
their sin and turn back to Him.

> *"Son of man, these men have set up idols in their hearts and put*
> *wicked stumbling blocks before their faces. Should I let them*

inquire of me at all? Therefore speak to them and tell them, 'This is what the Sovereign LORD *says: When any Israelite sets up idols in his heart and puts a wicked stumbling block before his face and then goes to a prophet, I the* LORD *will answer him myself in keeping with his great idolatry. I will do this to recapture the hearts of the people of Israel, who have all deserted me for their idols.'"*

(Ezekiel 14:3–5)

When we keep coming to God for Him to say yes when He has already said no, then it is a sure sign of some idol we are pursuing or is pressuring us. This is seen so tragically in the story of Balaam (Numbers 22:21–35). Balak, the king of the Moabites, wanted to hire him to curse the Israelites after hearing what had happened to the Egyptians and all the other armies they had defeated. So he sent some of the *"elders of Moab"* to Balaam with a fee for divination to curse God's people. Balaam should have had nothing to do with them, but he told them to stay the night and he would seek God.

God says to Balaam, *"Who are these men with with you?"* He was asking the prophet to explain himself and tells him emphatically he is to have nothing to do with them. Balaam recounts what God has told him and tells the messengers to return home, *"For the* LORD *has refused to let me go with you."*

They return home and report to their king but Balak does not give up and sends princes even more distinguished who come and plead with Balaam. They also promise a handsome reward and Balaam is made to feel more and more important. He gives what sounds like a very spiritual answer but something in his heart is being captured, *"Even if Balak gave me his palace filled with silver and gold, I could not do anything . . . to go beyond the command of the* LORD *my God. Now stay here tonight . . . and I will find out what else the* LORD *will tell me."*

God had already told Balaam to have nothing to do with their request. Yet this time when Balaam enquires he is told he can go, but must only do what God tells him. What's going on? Balaam is being answered according the idol he has set up in his heart.

In the morning Balaam saddles his donkey and goes with the princes but we are told, *"God was very angry when he went, and the angel of* LORD *stood in the road to oppose Him."* Balaam had become so spiritually deceived, that his donkey could see in the spiritual realm what he couldn't – an angel with a drawn sword blocking his way causing the animal to crush the prophet's foot against a wall. Balaam beats the donkey. He is angry because he is being made to look so foolish in front of the Moab princes. Here was this "great man" they needed being made to look stupid by a donkey. He is about to lash out once more when God speaks through the animal. Now the Moab princes look across and see the prophet having a conversation with a dumb animal. Then the Lord opens his eyes and he sees the angel of the Lord standing in his way with his sword drawn. He is told the donkey saved his life, for if he had not turned away he would have been killed. Balaam cries out, *"I have sinned . . . I will go back."* But God says he is to go with them but to only speak what He tells him.

What is happening in this prophet's heart? We are given a clear insight in 2 Peter 2:15: *"They have left the straight way and wandered off to follow the way of Balaam son of Beor, who loved the wages of wickedness."* Money and an exalted sense of his own importance had captured Balaam's heart. He couldn't curse the Israelites because God had blessed them, yet we see the state of his heart when he gives Balak a way to defeat them by enticing God's people to eat food sacrificed to idols and committing sexual immorality. This was Jesus' judgment on the church at Pergamum:

> *"Nevertheless, I have a few things against you: You have people there who hold to the teaching of Balaam, who taught Balak to entice the Israelites to sin by eating food sacrificed to idols and by committing sexual immorality."*   (Revelation 2:14)

Even a prophet can be seduced by an idol set up in their heart and so can great kings.

Numbering the fighting men

There was a time in King David's life when he fell into the same trap. There are two accounts in Scripture of his command for the fighting men of Israel to be numbered. They seem to be totally contradictory. The first is at the end of the second book of Samuel where God tells David to make a census of the nation's warriors (2 Samuel 24:1–4). But in the first book of Chronicles we read that Satan incited David to do this (1 Chronicles 21:1–5).

God was the nation's protection not the strength of their army. David above all should have known this for he had written, *"Some trust in chariots and some in horses, but we trust in the name of the* L*ORD* *our God"* (Psalm 20:7). We really don't know all that was going on in the deep places in David's heart but we do know that God was angry with him. It may have been David's pride or insecurity. He certainly asserted his authority by overruling Joab's plea not to do such a thing. David was listening to no one but his own desire. He ruled a great kingdom. He was a great king. Had it become an idol within his heart?

Almost a year is taken to count and number the men, and when David receives the results of the census the terrible consequences of his actions hit him like a thunderbolt. He cries out that he has sinned greatly and done a very foolish thing. God gives him three options: three years of famine, three months swept away by his enemies or three days of plague – *"the sword of the* L*ORD"*. He must choose one as a punishment. In deep distress he asks to fall into the hands of the Lord and three terrifying days of death came on the nation. They were so terrible that God commanded the judging angel to withhold his hand, seventy thousand men lay slain and David is humbled and repentant. He had discovered that every idol exacts a terrible cost.

Chapter 5

The Dangers of a Divided Heart

In one Peanuts cartoon Lucy says to Charlie Brown, "I hate everything. I hate everybody. I hate the whole wide world!" Charlie says, "But I thought you had inner peace." Lucy replies, "I do have inner peace. But I still have outer obnoxiousness"

One of the saddest stories I have read in recent years is what happened to one of the great church and prayer leaders of the 1980s. This man had a powerful ministry but sadly due to illness, spiritual attack and his own weakness things started going wrong. His ex-wife gave a very moving account in *Charisma* magazine of what happened as she spoke of his battle with depression and the intense pressures he was under. She summed it up, "Even though he started an affair with another woman I also believe he still loved me. What really happened was his heart became divided."[1]

When I read that I felt an overwhelming sense of sorrow and warning. No one who loves and serves God wakes up one morning and says, "Today I am going to commit adultery." All backsliding and especially "major" sin issues begin with a divided heart. It's not that you stop loving your spouse, but another is allowed to come alongside in your affections. All the devil's strongholds begin with footholds. You don't stop loving God but sin gets into the heart to divide and conquer. A kingdom divided cannot stand and neither can a divided heart.

I recently went through the entire Bible noting the number of times God says we are to love, obey, follow and trust Him wholeheartedly or with all our heart. Here is just a small selection.

*"But if from there you seek the LORD your God, you will find him if you look for him with all your **heart** and with all your soul."*

(Deuteronomy 4:29)

*"For the eyes of the LORD range throughout the earth to strengthen those whose **hearts** are fully committed to him."*

(2 Chronicles 16:9)

*"Trust in the LORD with all your **heart**
and lean not on your own understanding."*   (Proverbs 3:5)

*" 'Even now,' declares the LORD,
'return to me with all your **heart** . . . ' "*   (Joel 2:12)

The greatest prayer of the Jewish faith is the Shema:

*"Hear, O Israel, The LORD our God, the LORD is one. Love the LORD your God with all your **heart** and with all your soul and with all your strength."*   (Deuteronomy 6:4–5)

It was to be memorized by all Jews and recited liturgically by pious Jews twice each day.

Jesus summed up the whole law and commandments:

*"Love the Lord your God with all your **heart** and with all your soul and with all your mind and with all your strength."*

(Mark 12:30)

Joshua and Caleb were the only two out of 600,000 fighting men to enter the Promised Land because they alone followed the Lord wholeheartedly (Numbers 32:11). They had all walked through the Red Sea, seen the miracles and eaten the Manna, but every day for forty years three hundred of them died in the desert. What takes us into our destiny isn't only the dynamic encounters and miracles, but a continual keeping of our hearts right before God.

When Isaac Watts wrote, "When I survey the Wondrous Cross" he did it with simplicity and insight that has made his hymn one of the most loved and best known throughout the world. In his last verse he tells us what our response must be to such amazing love:

"Were the whole realm of nature mine
That were an offering far too small;
Love so amazing so divine
Demands my soul, my life, my all."

Seeing God

God reveals Himself to those who seek Him with all their heart. It isn't that He doesn't want to be found, but in the seeking we are changed to be able to see what is revealed to us. Jesus says, "It is the pure in heart that will see God" (Matthew 5:8). The word "pure" has two main meanings:

▶ *The first meaning is to be without any hint of hypocrisy or duplicity.*

The Jewish humorist Sam Levenson told the story of a driver who put a note under the windscreen wiper of a parked car. It read, "I have just smashed into your car. The people who saw the accident are watching me. They think I'm writing down my name and address. I'm not. Good luck." We may smile but this is the complete opposite of what Jesus meant. It was what he accused the Pharisees and other religious leaders of doing because they loved the praises of men more than of God. He said they were like white-washed sepulchers, shining bright on the outside but inside full of death and decay. They worshiped God with their lips but their hearts were far from Him.

He taught that true holiness is a heart issue:

> "... 'What goes into a man's mouth does not make him "unclean", but what comes out of his mouth, that is what makes him "unclean" ... Don't you see that whatever enters the mouth goes into the stomach and then out of the body? But the things that come out of the mouth come from the heart, and these make a man "unclean". For out of the heart come evil thoughts, murder, adultery, sexual immorality, theft, false testimony, slander. These are what make a man "unclean"; but eating with unwashed hands does not make him "unclean".'"
>
> (Matthew 15:10, 17–20)

William Barclay, commenting on these words says:

> "It may well be held that for a Jew this was the most startling thing Jesus ever said. For in this saying he condemns the Scribal and Pharisaic ritual and ceremonial religion. Jesus cancels the food laws of the Old Testament as having any spiritual power. They still stand as matters of health and hygiene but not as matters of religion. The

Scribes and Pharisees identified spirituality and pleasing God, with the observance of rules and regulations that had to do with cleanness and with uncleanness, with what a man ate and how he washed his hands before he ate it. Once and for all Jesus lays it down that what matters is not the state of a man's ritual observance, but the state of a man's heart.''

► *The other meaning of "purity" is to be clean, free from corruption and defilement.*

The word was used to describe corn winnowed and cleansed of all chaff and a metal free from all impurities with no alloy or mixture. To be pure in heart is to be both undefiled and undivided. It means that I am not one thing to your face and another behind your back. I don't sing like an angel in church and scream like a demon at home.

A divided heart always leads to a double mind, and a double-minded man is unstable in all his ways. Part of him rises up in faith while another is filled with doubt and unbelief. One moment he is trusting in God's provision while the next he is terrified about the future. He volunteers to serve but never shows up. He desperately desires to be holy and yet is frequently full of lust. He hates sin and loves it at the same time. What is wrong? It's a divided heart and a double mind. This is how Christians live with double standards and excuse them.

This is why James says:

> *"Come near to God and he will come near to you. Wash your hands, you sinners, and purify your hearts, you double-minded. Grieve, mourn and wail. Change your laughter to mourning and your joy to gloom. Humble yourselves before the Lord, and he will lift you up.''* (James 4:8–10)

Let me finish this chapter with a parable. It's not one you will find in the Bible but it is true to Scripture and to living a victorious life.

There was once a man who lived in a huge mansion with over fifty rooms. Jesus came to his home and the man gladly invited Him in and gave Him the biggest room. Immediately that room was filled with light and joy and peace. The next day there was another knock at the door. This time it was the devil. He wanted to come in and the man said no, but all day there was a terrible battle until at the end of it the man, exhausted, managed to finally shut the door. He was glad the devil was kept out but he was confused. Wasn't Jesus in the house? Why hadn't He come and helped him deal with things? So he decided to give Jesus more of the mansion and said the whole top floor is yours. Jesus filled it with His presence and His life.

The next day the devil came to call again and another terrible battle took place but finally he was kept out and turned away. The man came running to Jesus and wanted to know where He was? Jesus replied, "You invited Me into your house as a guest and gave Me a beautiful room but you didn't give Me all of them. Then you gave Me the whole top floor but still I was not given the whole house. Why don't you give Me all of the house? And then instead of Me just living with you, you will be living with Me." The man understood and with a big smile on his face he gave Jesus the key to the door and the deeds of the entire house. Jesus had access everywhere. The next day the devil came knocking at the door full of anger, prepared for an even longer fight. This time Jesus answered the door.

Chapter 6

Healing the Wounded Heart

If we all acted the way we really felt, four out of eight people at a dinner table would be sitting there sobbing.[1]
(Actor and comedian Jim Carrey)

The human heart is incredibly strong but it is also very vulnerable and fragile. Spiritually and emotionally the heart is no different. It has the capacity to empower to great accomplishments and sustain us through severe trials. But it is also very delicate, easily bruised and wounded. This is why words can inflict such terrible damage. A child punched in the face may get a black eye which disappears within a week, but call them fat and tell them no one loves them and you can cause damage that lasts a lifetime.

This is also the reason why emotional pain can be far more unbearable than physical pain. A person may be able to stand almost any attack on their body, but what finally breaks them is a broken heart. William Barclay tells the story that during the rule of Hitler's terror in Germany, a man was arrested, tried and tortured and put into a concentration camp. He bore the torment of his accusers with great strength and determination and remained unbroken. Then by accident he discovered who it was who had informed against him, it was his own son. This broke him and soon after he died.[2]

It is said that when Julius Caesar was murdered he faced his assassins with almost disdainful courage. But when he saw his friend Brutus raise his hand to strike, he wrapped his head in his cloak and died.[3]

This is even more dramatically portrayed in the blockbuster film *Braveheart* starring Mel Gibson. I jokingly tell people I have seen most of it three times. It is a powerful picture but gory in parts. Like almost all Hollywood portrayals of history it stretches and massages the truth to make a good script, but the basis of the story finds its roots in Scottish history.

About halfway through the film the English and Scottish armies face each other with the Scots greatly outnumbered, but "Braveheart" William Wallace leads the charge and is seen running into battle with his huge sword engaging the enemy. It is a bloody scene portraying the full horror of battle. During the conflict Wallace gives chase after the English king and one of the knights guarding the king is told to turn back and engage the attacker. The two fight each other and Braveheart is thrown from his horse and lies motionless on the ground. When the king's defender gets down from his horse to inspect his defeated foe, he is surprised and thrown to the ground as Braveheart tricks him and holds a knife to his throat. He pulls the helmet off the helpless knight and to his astonishment sees it is Robert the Bruce, who had sided with the English. In that moment everything stands still as Braveheart comes to terms with what this means. The man he was fighting for has betrayed him. All he can do is lie back on the ground paralysed by the pain and the shock. He doesn't care that English soldiers are charging up behind to capture and kill him. All the fight and passion has been knocked out of him.

Of course the film has a long way to go and he is rescued, but that one moment shows how a "Braveheart" can become a "Brokenheart" and the devastating effect it has. The great warrior is crushed and defeated not by an English sword but by one of his own countrymen's betrayal. Broken hearts destroy life just as much as broken bodies – sometimes even more.

Being betrayed is so profoundly painful few people can talk about it, yet if they do open up you can't stop the flow of hurt and anguish. What makes the pain so terrible is that someone who knows your heart and character turns against you and even chooses to believe the worst about you. The mind freezes as it then tries to grasp how a friend or a spouse, a child, a colleague, a parent could do or say what they have. Someone who knew you deeply and intimately has turned on you and attacked you. The singer and songwriter Michael Card powerfully captures the agony in one of his songs when he says, "Only a friend can betray a friend, a stranger has nothing to gain. And only a friend comes close enough to ever cause so much pain." David understood this when he spoke about his own betrayal:

"If an enemy were insulting me,
*   I could endure it;*
If a foe were raising himself against me,
*   I could hide from him.*
But it is you, a man like myself,
*   my companion, my close friend,*
with whom I once enjoyed sweet fellowship
*   as we walked with the throng at the house of God . . .*
My companion attacks his friends;
*   he violates his covenant.*
His speech is smooth as butter,
*   yet war is in his heart . . . "*   (Psalm 55:12–14, 20–21)

Perhaps the only other emotional pain greater than betrayal is the grief of bereavement and forsakenness. God knows what this is like. He bore it in a measure that was without limit. After three years of friendship and ministry Judas betrays Jesus for thirty silver coins, the price of a common slave. Jesus was denied, deserted, falsely accused, abused and tortured. He was stripped naked and hung on a cross to die. There is no pain or anguish we go through that Jesus doesn't understand. A spear was thrust into His side and out flowed blood and water. Medically this is the sign of a ruptured heart. Bearing the penalty of this world's sin literally broke God's heart.

Over one thousand years before David prophetically foretold the crucifixion, hundreds of years before such a death was invented.

"I am poured out like water,
*   and all my bones are out of joint.*
My heart has turned to wax;
*   it has melted away within me."*   (Psalm 22:14)

Our world is filled with pain and Jesus understands your pain. He knows not only the facts but also the feelings. He knows the anxiety, the anguish, the abandonment, loneliness, isolation and rejection, "He is touched with the feelings of our infirmities" (Hebrews 4:15).

When a young and beautiful athletic Joni Earackson Tada struck a rock one-day as she dived into a lake, paralysis resulted and she became quadraplegic. Her witness has now become worldwide through her books and ministry and the movie of her life, but the early years were filled with unbearable pain.

Joni realised how really helpless she was one night when she begged a friend to give her some pills so she could die. When her friend refused she thought, "I can't even die on my own!" At first life was hell. Pain, rage, bitterness and emotional anguish shook her spirit. Although she couldn't really feel physical pain, piercing sensations racked her nerves and ran through her body. This went on for three years.

One night there came a dramatic change in Joni that now makes her the beautiful, radiant Christian she is. Her best friend, Cindy, was at her bedside searching desperately for some way to encourage her. It must have come from the Holy Spirit, for she suddenly blurted it out, "Joni, Jesus knows how you feel. You're not the only one who's been paralyzed. He was paralyzed too."

Joni glared at her. "Cindy, what are you talking about?"

"It's true, it's true, Joni. Remember that He was nailed to the cross. His back was raw from beatings like your back sometimes gets raw. Oh, He must have longed to move. To change His position, to redistribute His weight somehow, but He couldn't move. Joni, He knows how you feel."

The thought intrigued and gripped Joni and for a moment, took her mind off her own pain. It had never occurred to her that God might have felt the same piercing sensations that now racked her body and Jesus knew the helplessness she suffered. The realisation was profoundly comforting.

Joni discovered that night the reality of the words found in Psalm 34:18:

> *"The LORD is close to the brokenhearted*
> *and saves those who are crushed in spirit."*

She said, "God became incredibly close to me."[4]

"I'm going fishing"

These were the words of a man with a broken heart. He had seen Jesus risen from the dead, but the emotional roller coaster of the past weeks and his own personal sense of failure in denying Jesus, were more than he could bear. He had heard the words of the women who said that Jesus told them to *"go, tell his disciples and Peter,"* but even that seemed to highlight not only how much Jesus loved him but also how he had so badly failed such love.

Now more than a week after Jesus had first appeared to His disciples Peter turns to some of them and says, *"I'm going fishing"* and several of them respond, *"I'm coming too."* Nothing so remarkable about that you would think until you examine what those words really convey. I am indebted to the insights of Greek scholar Kenneth Wuest in his word studies of the New Testament.[5]

The words *"I'm going"* are the translation of the Greek word *hupago*, which is used to denote the final departure of one who ceases to be another's companion or attendant. In other words they mean, "this is the end, it's over, time for separate ways". This was Peter's formal announcement that he had had enough and he was breaking relations with Jesus as far as any future service and ministry were concerned.

The word "fishing" is the translation of the present infinitive of the verb *halieuo*, which implies action is durative, progressive and constantly ongoing. Peter is saying, "I'm going back to the family business and what I know best." Six of the other disciples respond, *"We are coming with you."* Again the Greek word for "coming" does not refer merely to the act of simply going along with someone, but in such a context includes the idea of joining in that person's decision.

These expert fishermen fished all night and caught nothing. In the morning sunlight Jesus is standing on the shore yet they do not recognise Him. He calls to them asking if they have caught any fish, but the question in the original language indicates the person asking it expects the answer to be no. They are told to throw the net out again on the other side and this time they catch a huge haul of fish. At this moment John immediately knows that this is the Lord and Peter, having lost none of his impetuousness, jumps out of the boat and wades towards the shore.

If you were Jesus what would you say to these men you had invested your life in and given your life for? These disciples on whom so much depended, who preferred to go back to catching fish instead of changing the world. They all knew who He was but none of them dared show it. Jesus, aware of their pain and confusion, simply says, "Come and have something to eat, I've just cooked breakfast." After this He calls Peter to one side and they walk along the seashore.

Three times Peter had denied Him and three times Jesus asks

one simple heart searching question, *"[Peter], do you love me?"*
Two different words are used for love in the conversation and
Jesus begins by asking, *"Do you truly love me more than these?"* The
word Jesus uses for love is *agapao,* the deepest expression of love
that is willing to give one's all and even lay down your life. Peter,
aware of how he had failed to do this even after saying, *"If
everyone else denies you I never will,"* answers Jesus and says, *"Yes,
Lord, you know that I love you,"* but the word he uses for "love" is
not *agape* it is *phileo* a love of deep friendship and affection. Jesus
asks again if Peter loves Him with a love that is willing to give his
all and Peter responds with a love that expresses great fondness
and affection. Once more Jesus asks Peter if he loves Him but this
time He uses the same word as Peter has been using, *phileo,*
"Peter, do you really have a deep affection for me?" Jesus had
been asking for a love of deep devotion and Peter had been
answering with a love of deep emotion, but now Jesus even
questions this and Peter is grieved because the pain of the failure
and denial is being opened fully.

Jesus says, *"[I know you love me, Peter and I know how much
you love, I have always seen in you more than you knew
yourself.] When you were younger you dressed yourself and went
where you wanted; but when you are old* [there will come a day
when] *you will stretch out your hands, and someone else will dress you
and lead where you do not want to go."* John tells us Jesus said this
to indicate the kind of death by which Peter would glorify God.
More than thirty years later Peter was martyred and historians
tell us that when he was about to be crucified he said, "I am not
worthy to die as my Lord," so they crucified him upside down.

When Peter denied Jesus it was his Galilean accent that gave
him away. Galileans spoke with a rough burr that was considered
course and unrefined. No Galilean was allowed to pronounce the
benediction at a synagogue service. Life's experiences declared
Peter a failure and even religion forbade him to close a service in
prayer, but when Jesus restored him and the Holy Spirit filled
him, the whole world felt the impact. It was this rough unrefined
tongue that uttered the amazing words, *"You are the Christ, the
Son of the living God."* It was from Peter's mouth that the words
poured out on the Day of Pentecost and 3,000 were saved and
added to the church.

Peter the broken shepherd became the pastor and leader of the
Early Church. The very place we have been most broken and
wounded can become the place from which God will use us to

minister to others. Where we have received grace, is from where we are able to release it to bring God's healing to others. When Paul gave the signs of his apostolic authority he mentioned among them his scars. The place of wounding and brokenness that Jesus took for us has become the source from which our healing and salvation flow, *"... by his wounds we are healed"* (Isaiah 53:5).

Jonathan Edwards was one of the greatest theologians and preachers the church has had in the past thousand years. During his time at Northampton, New England during the eighteenth century, he was instrumental in two revivals. Dr Martyn Lloyd-Jones referred to him in the following manner, while addressing the Westminster Puritan Conference in 1976:

> "Now let us look at this man who has had such a lasting influence ... Indeed I am tempted, perhaps foolishly, to compare the Puritans to the Alps, Luther and Calvin to the Himalayas, and Jonathan Edwards to Mount Everest! He has always seemed to me to be the man most like the Apostle Paul ... He stands out, it seems to me, quite on his own amongst men."[6]

In 1727 he was ordained as assistant pastor to his grandfather, Solomon Stoddart, in the town of Northampton, Massachusetts. Within a year or so the old man had died and Edwards became the sole pastor. There he remained for the next twenty-three years until 1750 when he was literally turned out of his church.

Lloyd-Jones comments:

> "This was one of the most amazing things that ever happened, and it should come as a word of encouragement to ministers and preachers. Here was this towering genius, this mighty preacher, this man at the center of a great revival – yet he was literally voted out of his church by 230 votes against 23. Do not be surprised then, brethren, as to what may happen to you in your churches."[7]

The main reason for his dismissal was over who was allowed to partake of "the Lord's Table". Edwards had become deeply concerned about the spiritual apathy and worldliness that was evident among many in the town and even his own church. He sought to address this by making it clear that partaking at the Lord's Table was a great honor for those whose hearts and lives were in right standing with God. He proposed that none be admitted to do so but those who, after due examination, were regarded as in right standing with God, through Jesus Christ. This caused a storm and "the town was put into a great ferment; and before he was heard in his own defence, or it was known by many what his principles were, the general cry was to have him dismissed."[8]

His farewell sermon has been described as the greatest farewell sermon ever preached. There was no trace of bitterness or resentment for the way he had been treated, as every sentence seems to have been spoken in meekness and forgiveness. He finished his message:

> "I now take my leave of you, and bid you all farewell; wishing and praying for your best prosperity. I would commend your immortal souls to Him, who formerly committed them to me, expecting the day when I must meet you again before Him, who is the Judge of the quick and the dead. I desire that I may never forget this people, who have been so long my special charge, and that I may never cease fervently to pray for your prosperity."[9]

For almost the next year he was without a pastorate and his letters make moving reading as he describes the struggles and the difficulties he went through. He had a large family to support and his age and dismissal meant that there were few opportunities offered him for further ministry. Yet his writings are full of God's goodness and the humility of a man who bore no grudge or resentment. Indeed, on a few occasions his old church asked if he would take a Sunday service because they could find no one to replace him, and he graciously ministered to the people who had so unfairly dismissed him.

When a call did come for a new appointment it was far away from fashionable Boston to a frontier town amongst the Indians at Stockbridge. Here he pastored over two hundred Indians on the reservation and another church in the area. Busy though he was it still left him with more free time than he had ever known in Boston where it seems the devil had sought to consume his time and health with endless arguments and problems. Now Edwards was free to write, and from this lonely frontier place, God through him, gave us some of the ablest and most valuable works the church of Christ has in its possession.[10]

From the place of your deepest wounding, grace can also flow to others as you allow the Lord to heal your heart. What the devil intended to destroy you, God is able to make become your most powerful ministry.

Many years ago, in a mental institution outside Boston, a young girl known as "Little Annie" was locked in the dungeon. The dungeon was the only place, said the doctors, for those who were hopelessly insane. In Little Annie's case they saw no hope for her, so she was consigned to a living death in that small cage that received little light and even less hope. About that time, an elderly nurse was nearing retirement. She felt there was hope for all of God's children, so she started taking her lunch into the dungeon and eating outside Little Annie's cage. She felt perhaps she should communicate some love and hope to the small child.

In many ways, Little Annie was like an animal. On occasions, she would violently attack the person who came into her cage. At other times, she would completely ignore them. When the elderly nurse started visiting her, Little Annie gave no indication that she was even aware of her presence.

One day, the elderly nurse brought some chocolate cakes to the dungeon and left them outside the cage. Little Annie gave no hint she knew they were there, but when the nurse returned the next day, the brownies were gone. From that time on, the nurse would bring cakes when she made her Thursday visit. Soon after, the doctors in the institution noticed a change was taking place. After a period of time they decided to move Little Annie upstairs. Finally, the day came when the "hopeless case" was told she could return home. But Little Annie did not wish to leave. She chose to stay, to help others. She understood their pain and desperation better than all the doctors and nurses.

Sometime later she was asked to care for another little girl who because of an illness became deaf, mute and blind by the age of two. They thought no one could get through to this child but Annie did and the small girl Helen Keller, became famous as she grew up to give lectures and insights that astonished our world because her nurse Annie Sullivan never gave up and knew there was hope. Science has made great advances in the treatment of pain relief but where do you go with a broken heart?

PART TWO

Setting a Guard

Chapter 7

Keep Your Heart Soft

*It doesn't matter how good the seed is
if the soil is unresponsive.*

One of the most quoted preachers of the past century was the Southern Baptist minister, Vance Havner. Many times provocative, often profound and frequently funny. Here is just a small selection of his quotes.

"The church is so subnormal that if it ever got back to normal if would seem to people to be abnormal."

"Put more fire into your sermons or put more of your sermons into the fire."

"Jesus knows we must come apart and rest a while or else we may just plain come apart."

"Our world is fast becoming a mad house and the inmates are trying to run the asylum. It is a strange time when the patients are writing the prescriptions, the students threatening to run the schools and church members and not the Holy Spirit to direct the Church."

"Too much of our orthodoxy is correct and sound, but like words without a tune, it does not glow and burn; it does not stir the heart; it has lost its hallelujah. One man with a genuine glowing experience with God is worth a library full of arguments."

"The problem with the typical morning worship service is that it starts at 11 o'clock sharp and ends at 12 o'clock dull."[1]

But the quote I like the most is what he said about being involved in Christian service:

> "In ministry you need the mind of a scholar, the heart of a child and the hide of a rhinoceros."

After more than twenty years of being a pastor I shout a loud "Amen" to that. I also take the liberty of adding, "We must learn how to keep our hide hard and our hearts soft." Tragically because of the pressures and hurts of life, many develop soft hides and hard hearts.

In the Parable of the Sower (Matthew 13) the seed is always the same and so is the sower, but what determines the flow of life and whether or not there is a harvest is the receptivity of the soil. It doesn't matter how good the sower or the seed is, unless it is sown in good soil it will never produce a good harvest. Jesus explained in detail what He meant and warns us of the three things that stop us becoming producers of spiritual life. But before we look at them we need to understand a little bit of background.

The picture of a sower would have been familiar to Jesus' hearers, and even as He told the story there may well have been such a person sowing in one of the fields nearby. In Palestine there were two ways of sowing seed. There was the lazy way when a bag of seed was placed on the back of a donkey. A hole was cut in the corner of the sack and the animal was walked up and down the field. The other method was for a person to carry the seed and throw it out as they walked along. This was more accurate but even then the wind could catch it and blow it to all kinds of places.

Often the fields were long narrow strips and the ground between them was a right of way that became a well-trodden path beaten hard under foot. There was also stony ground, which was very common with a thin skin of earth on top of an underlying shelf of limestone rock. The seed here would germinate very quickly, grow rapidly in the warm sun but soon die. There was also an abundance of thorny ground that looked quite deceptive. It appeared clean but contained weeds and fibrous roots and pests. The good ground was deep, clean and soft.

► *The seed that fell on the path*
This seed was eaten by the birds that quickly swooped down to devour it. This is likened to a direct attack of the devil who steals

God's word from us because even though it is heard, it is not understood.

▶ *The seed that fell among thorns and thistles*
This seed was choked to death. Its life was strangled by plants and weeds that symbolize the worries of life and the deceitfulness of wealth.

▶ *The seed that fell on rocky places*
This seed did not have much soil and even though it would spring up quickly, when the sun came out and trials came the plants quickly withered away.

There is no harvest except for the seed that fell on good soil. The path, the thorns and thistles and rocky places all had one thing in common, there was no depth, only a superficial shallowness. Only the good soil had depth.

As you listen to Jesus' words describing how the kingdom of God operates, you are inevitably drawn to the conclusion that the soil is referring to a person's heart.

> *"Though seeing, they do not see;*
> *though hearing, they do not hear or understand.*

> *In them is fulfilled the prophecy of Isaiah:*

> *'You will be ever hearing but never understanding;*
> *you will be ever seeing but never perceiving.*
> *For this people's heart has become calloused;*
> *they hardly hear with their ears,*
> *and they have closed their eyes.*
> *Otherwise they might see with their eyes,*
> *hear with their ears,*
> *understand with their hearts*
> *and turn, and I would heal them.'"*   (Matthew 13:13–15)

Even though God knew they would not respond to Him because of their hardened hearts, He loved them so much He still wanted them to hear. Information is about the head but understanding and revelation of spiritual truth has to do with the heart. This is why Paul says to the church at Ephesus, *"I pray also that the eyes of your heart may be enlightened in order that you may know the hope to which he has called you, the riches of his glorious inheritance in the saints"* (Ephesians 1:18).

I love theology because it is the study of God, but the danger of it can be that you mistake getting to know about Him for truly getting to know Him. Such study will always have its limitations because we are not seeking to understand a power or principle but a person. A small child or uneducated peasant will have more understanding of God through revelation and relationship than the greatest theologian and academic will ever know by simply study and research. Anyway, how could we ever get to truly know what God is like by our limited reasoning and understanding, after all He is Almighty?

Three symptoms of a hardened heart

A whole generation of Israelites who walked through the Red Sea never set foot in the Promised Land. Every day for forty years those who died were being buried. There was a constant funeral procession and the sound of wailing in the camp.

In the book of Hebrews chapters 3 and 4 we are told the reason they did not enter God's promise and provision for their lives. Three times we read, "They heard God's voice and hardened their hearts." A hard heart will desensitise you to the voice of God but a soft heart makes you spiritually perceptive.

1. Rebellious and restless

A young child was repeatedly told by his father to sit down on the back seat of the car. He defiantly remained standing until his dad physically sat him down. The small lad grinned and muttered, "I may be sitting down on the outside but I am still standing up on the inside." Rebellion is an inside job.

The night Moses was receiving the Ten Commandments from God with the very first *"to have no other gods before me"*, the people were making a golden calf to worship. They did not want to rebel against Pharaoh who enslaved them but complained constantly and rose up against Moses and God who had delivered them.

Rebellion always leads to restlessness, never at peace, never satisfied, never content, always finding fault and wandering in your own personal desert. It is one thing to go through a wilderness experience, we all do from time to time, but it's tragic to wander around in it until you die.

2. Unbelieving and ungrateful

One military strategist catalogued the human impossibility and immensity of the Israelites deliverance from Egypt:

- There was a minimum of two million people who were to leave, quite a task when you consider the difficulty involved in securing political asylum for just one person today.

- Egypt was the most fortified country known then. It was bounded on its western side by desert and on its eastern side by a line of fortresses that were designed not only to keep an aggressor out, but also to keep the population in. To the south it was protected by the Red Sea. Egypt also had an understanding with its neighboring territories that any fugitives from her should be returned.

- The route to be taken was via one of the most desolate deserts in the world.

- Nine hundred tons of food would be required to sustain the people and livestock each day.

- Two thousand four hundred tons of firewood would be required for cooking.

- Two million gallons of water would be needed to satisfy the thirst of both animals and men – and that in a desert that had become so, through lack of water![2]

We read in Psalm 105:37 (NIV), *"He brought out Israel, laden with silver and gold, and from among their tribes no one faltered."* Other translations say not one of them was *"feeble or sick"*. The Hebrew word *kashal* means "a totterer or stumbler". C.H. Spurgeon comments, "The number of their army was very great and yet there was not one in hospital, not one carried in an ambulance or limping in the rear. Jehovah Rophi had healed them; they carried none of the diseases of Egypt with them and felt none of the exhaustion which sore bondage produces. See the contrast between Egypt and Israel – in Egypt one dead in every house, and among the Israelites not so much as limping."[3] The Bible commentator Matthew Henry says, "They came all out in good health, there was not one sick."

It is truly amazing that among so many, not one was infirm or unable to make the journey. All the Israelites had known was slavery, their diet and health care were minimal. Just before they left Egypt it had been worse, much worse, with the full fury of Pharaoh demanding "bricks without straw".

The population of Wales where I live is about the same number as those which came out of Egypt. It is a good place to live with its health care and provision yet the hospitals are full. Too many to count would never have made it out of Egypt into the hot desert wilderness and many of those who did would not have survived for long. What joy would it be if you were an Israelite knowing your time of freedom had come, but you had to leave loved ones behind because they were too old and feeble or knowing they were being taken to certain death in the scorching desert sun?

So what happened?
On the night of Passover as death came into Egyptian houses, life and healing came into the homes of the Israelites. The blood above the doorposts not only protected the Israelite from the power of death, but also brought life among them as they ate the Passover lamb. Paul tells us that Jesus is our Passover Lamb and that first Passover spoke of something greater to come. He also warns us that if we eat and drink unworthily not discerning the Lord's body, then sickness and even death can result. If there is a power released to bring death how much more to bring life. This is why the Communion Table is a place of healing not only spiritually but also physically and emotionally.

That first Passover was an amazing miracle service. Yet amazingly their unbelief and ingratitude hardened them and what Pharaoh and his chariots couldn't do, a hard heart did. They died in the wilderness because *"the message they heard was of no value to them, because those who heard did not combine it with faith"* (Hebrews 4:2). Their hearts were too hard.

3. Confused and cynical
The Israelites said God is playing games with us, "He only brought us here to die." They attacked Moses' motives and even questioned God's.

There will be many experiences in life and church that will hurt and disappointed us and we have to ensure we keep our hearts soft – I know this is not always easy. When you have spent months and even years trying to help a person and they turn against you, hardness can creep in. When you go the extra mile to help someone and they pretend to be your friend, but behind your back they are scheming to harm you, the heart takes a pounding. When we have opened our heart to those who have walked all over it, we need the soothing oil of the Holy Spirit's love and healing to keep us soft, because it is not what happens to us that defeats us but what happens within us. A hardening of the attitudes destroys more lives than hardening of the arteries ever could. It is often said that all God is looking for is availability. I don't believe that. There are always those who make themselves available but their attitude disqualifies them.

The late David Watson wrote these powerful words regarding the heart:

"To love all is to be vulnerable. Love anything, and your heart will certainly be wrung and possibly broken. If you want to make sure of keeping it intact, you must give your heart to no one. Wrap it carefully round with hobbies and little luxuries; avoid all entanglements; lock it safe in a casket or coffin of your selfishness. But in that casket, safe, dark, motionless, airless, it will change. It will not be broken; it will become unbreakable, impenetrable, and irredeemable. The only place outside heaven where you can be perfectly safe from all the dangers of love is hell."[4]

Chapter 8

Forgive

Without forgiveness we die inside.

South Africa's Truth and Reconciliation Commission was set up following the demise of apartheid. During its investigations members of the Commission heard many harrowing accounts of abuses and atrocities that took place under that evil system. Yet as the name of the Commission suggests, the desire to establish the truth was not to drive the country apart but to seek healing and restoration. In one of the cases an elderly lady stood before them in the emotionally charged courtroom, listening to white police officers acknowledge the atrocities they had perpetrated. Officer van de Broek acknowledged his responsibility in the death of her son. Along with others, he had shot her eighteen-year-old son at point-blank range. He and the others partied while they burned his body, turning it over and over on the fire until it was reduced to ashes.

Eight years later, van de Broek and others arrived to seize her husband. A few hours later, shortly after midnight, van de Broek came to fetch the woman. He took her to a woodpile where her husband lay bound. She was forced to watch as they poured petrol over his body and ignited the flames that consumed him. The last words she heard her husband say were "Forgive them." Now, van de Broek stood before her awaiting judgment. The Commission asked her what she wanted.

"I want three things," she said calmly. "I want Mr van de Broek to take me to the place where they burned my husband's body. I would like to gather up the dust and give him a decent burial. Second, Mr van de Broek took all my family away from me, and I still have a lot of love to give. Twice a month, I would like for him to come to the ghetto and spend a day with me so I can be a mother to him. Third, I would like Mr van de Broek to know that God has forgiven him, and that I forgive him too. I would like someone to lead me to where he is seated, so I can embrace him and he can know my forgiveness is real."

As the elderly woman was led across the courtroom, van de Broek fainted, overwhelmed. Someone began singing "Amazing Grace". Gradually everyone joined in.[1]

During those bloodstained years of apartheid amazing acts of love and forgiveness were evidenced many times. Another moving account is that of Benjamin Dube recounted in Paul Estabrook's wonderful book, *Secrets to Spiritual Success*. Benjamin Dube was an evangelist who witnessed for Christ on the streets of Soweto. His message was that instead of hating and killing each other, blacks and whites must love one another. His life was threatened many times and one day some blacks approached him and warned him to stop preaching about love, "We don't want to love our neighbor, we hate them," they told him.

Benjamin carried on. One night he had a vivid dream in which he was stabbed to death by his own people. He woke up his wife, Grace, and told her he believed the dream would happen. The following day they discussed the dream and also the constant threats with their children. "Must I continue this message of forgiveness?" he asked them. They all nodded aware what the consequences might be. They then prayed together asking the Lord for strength to remain faithful. Not long afterwards Dube was out preaching again and his children were with him. In the middle of Soweto ten black men stopped his car. They dragged him out and stuck a knife into his chest sixteen times. The children fled with twelve-year-old Bonani hiding behind a rubbish bin. He watched helplessly as his father was repeatedly stabbed.

The murderers then took Benjamin's Bible, dipped it in his blood and disappeared into a dark street. When little Bonani got to his father he was already dead. He rushed home to tell his mother the horrible news. He ran into his bedroom and in great pain and sorrow cried out to God. He opened his Bible lying near by and the first words he read were of Jesus on the cross, *"Father forgive them, for they know not what they do."* He drew strength from the words and then and there composed a new music score to sing them. Later the murderers were arrested, seven of the ten were given just three months imprisonment because they had only helped plan the murder, but were not directly involved. The others were given fifteen years.

After the funeral, Grace and her children got together and decided they would not stop sharing their message of love and forgiveness. Together they sang and witnessed on the streets about the love of God. About a year after her husband's death something remarkable happened. As she and the children held an open-air meeting, she gave a call for those listening to give their lives to Christ. There was a lot of movement in the crowd as young and old came forward. Suddenly a man pushed through and stood with his head bowed before Grace Dube, "I also want to start a new life with Jesus," he said softly.

Grace looked at the young man and started to tremble. He was one of the seven accomplices who had planned the murder of her husband. He did not look at her and for a moment Grace did not know what to say. Then she put her arms around him and through her tears said, "Now you are my brother!"

A deathly silence had descended on the crowd. They recognised the man too, and so had Grace's children. While everyone looked on, the children began to sing, "What a mighty God we serve".[2]

Why is forgiveness so important?

Because without it we are locked into the pain of the past which causes us to die inside.

There are many Christians forgiven by God but who are never really sure of it, and one of the major reasons is they have never taken the steps to get rid of the bitterness and resentment they hold in their hearts towards others. The problem they experience in not feeling forgiven is not God's fault but their own. He has forgiven them on the basis of their own personal repentance, but His forgiveness is unable to reach the center of their spirit and dissolve the feelings of guilt because they harbor an unforgiving attitude towards others.

Forgiveness releases the grace of God not only to the villain but also to the victim. It sets us free and allows healing to take place. When we don't forgive we become a prisoner to what has been done to us and to those who have done it.

In his fascinating book *None of These Diseases* Dr S. McMillen writes:

"When people say through clenched teeth, 'I'll get even if it's the last thing I do,' it often is. The moment I start hating a man I become his slave. I can't enjoy my work anymore because he even controls my thoughts. My resentments produce too many stress hormones in my body and I become fatigued after only a few hours of work. The work I formerly enjoyed is now drudgery. Even holidays cease to give me pleasure. It may be a luxurious car that I drive along a lake fringed with the autumnal beauty of maple oak and birch. As far as my experience of pleasure is concerned, I might as well be driving a wagon in the mud and rain. The man I hate hounds me wherever I go. I can't escape his tyrannical grip on my mind. When the waiter serves me fillet stake with French fries and all the trimmings, and after strawberry cheesecake smothered in cream, it might as well be stale bread and water. My teeth chew the food and I swallow it, but the man I hate will not permit me to enjoy it. King Solomon understood this, 'Better a dish of vegetables with love, than the best beef served with hatred.'"

McMillen goes on to vividly and humorously describe the high cost in getting even by relating a story that Dale Carnegie recounts on a trip to Yellowstone Park, and a visit to the place where the Grizzly bears were fed:

"The guide told us that the grizzly could whip any animal in the West with the possible exceptions of the Buffalo and the Kadiak bear. As we watched we noticed there was only one other animal that the grizzly would allow to eat with him and take some of his food. It was the skunk. The guide explained that of course the grizzly could whip that old skunk and he resented him for taking his food and was maddened at the skunk's brazen impudence, but he let him alone. The reason why? Because that old bear was far smarter than most people, he knew there would be a high cost to getting even."

You may not have heard of the Russian poet Irina Ratushin-skaya, but her poetry expressing her faith in Christ brought inspiration and hope to believers all over the Soviet Union during the dark days of communist control. It also brought her to the attention of the KGB, and at age twenty-eight she was arrested and sentenced to seven years hard labor in the Bareshevo Work-camp. She was subjected to relentless interrogations, chilling cold, starvation, hard labor, and months of solitary confinement. Her faith did not break and her suffering actually brought her closer to God.

Speaking of her ordeals she said

"Those of us who have survived totalitarian prisons are endlessly asked, 'Why don't you sound bitter about the past?' When we try and explain that in a way it was a positive experience, people make strange faces and ask what is so positive about suffering? So I would like to share some of the lessons that I, and some of my friends learned in custody.

The first lesson one learns immediately after being arrested is about hatred. Those who are not able to throw their anger away simply become insane. In every day life if you are angry you can always think about something else, but the KGB did not allow this easy escape. The whole system was designed by psychologists in such a way that from the very beginning one had to cope with constant humiliation and blackmail. Problems usually started after a couple of days when one could not sleep. Everyone feels the need to escape from this anger and all of us who survived learned ways of doing this. For instance, when my interrogator told me that if I didn't speak he would kill my husband, the only thing I could think was that my interrogation could only last about a year, because I wasn't answering their questions. So in a year I would be out but my interrogator would be here forever. In other words what I am experiencing now will not last.

Secondly you can feel pity towards your interrogator. One can think, 'Look what the devil is doing to this person. He is enjoying himself. This means that he is in real danger.' So I had to do something for him not to let the devil snatch him away. I prayed for him. This is what I did during my interrogation. I have seen the power of prayer and forgiveness at work."

Footprints

Another lady you may not have heard of by name, but whose poem *Footprints* has become famous all over the world is Margaret Fishback Powers. She wrote the poem in 1964 after her boyfriend, Paul Powers, a children's evangelist asked her to marry him. He had been invited to speak at a youth conference north of Kingston, 100 miles east of Toronto, Canada. They arrived early and went for a walk on the nearby beach. They jumped out of the car, leaving behind their shoes, and went off barefoot, squishing the warm sand beneath their toes as they ran along. The setting sun dancing on the water made it sparkle. It was incredibly beautiful as they walked and talked about their future together serving God and the challenges that lay ahead of them. As the waves washed up over their footprints, they noticed they had left only one set of prints visible. Observing that Margaret said, "Maybe that's what will happen to us – maybe we'll be all washed up. Maybe our dreams are all going to wash away." "No," Paul protested, "this makes me think of our future. On our wedding day, we two will become one, and oh, the joy that will be mine to go with you throughout our life together. See our footprints just up ahead? They're still there. Where they got washed out is just the troubled waters we're going to face. Every marriage faces that."

She was still apprehensive, "Will we have what it takes to weather the troubled waters?" Paul stopped, looked deep into her eyes and promised, "We'll have it. If we love each other enough to fight for what we have, we'll make it." "What will happen when trouble comes that we just can't handle?" she asked. Paul sighed and was silent for a moment. His grip on her hand tightened reassuringly and he said, "Margie, when the most troublesome times come that neither one of us can handle, that's when the Lord will carry us both, as long as we maintain our faith and trust in Him." It was those words and an experience she had that night when as if in a dream she saw herself walking along a beach with her Lord, which inspired her to write the poem about footprints in the sand.

Margaret married Paul and they served the Lord together. Sixteen years later in July 1980 they moved to British Columbia where Paul was hired to do promotional work for Dr James Dobson's new *Focus on the Family* films. During the move all her poems, songs and letters went missing. The removal company had lost the six boxes containing all her precious work. They said they would search their warehouse, but the boxes were not found and then the company went bankrupt.

Three years later she and Paul were in Holland attending a conference for itinerant evangelists, hosted by the Billy Graham evangelistic organization. Passing through the state of

Washington on the way home, they came across calligraphy of the *Footprints* poem in a Christian bookstore. Margaret says she was dumbfounded and shocked. They purchased the plaque to compare it with her poem and it was almost identical. The woman purporting to be the author had her name and address on the back and Margaret says, "I immediately wrote her asking for an explanation." The woman's husband responded by stating they would never steal anything and for her to stop harassing them.

This began a period of unbelievable stress. Later they went back to that bookstore and found a dozen other poems she had written and that had been lost by the removal company, all done in calligraphy on plaques. She wrote to the woman and her husband again – no response. After repeated letters to them were returned unopened, she gave up the effort. Several weeks later, doing ministry work on Vancouver Island they came across the poem again in a bookstore in Victoria. This time it was entitled, *I Had a Dream*, her original title. She noted it was published by a major US publishing company. She wrote to them and hired a copyright lawyer in Vancouver. All her poems were copyrighted at lawyers in Toronto. The publisher skirted the issue saying they needed more proof, and so it went on and became a legal nightmare.

It seems everywhere they went they came across the poem. One woman wrote her autobiography, in which she claimed God had given her the poem. She even set it to music. Everyone Margaret wrote to made no difference, people were making too much money from it. She became frustrated, angry, stressed, jealous and felt abused and outraged. Something was eating away at her. She had to get rid of the anger but didn't know how. She was becoming full of bitterness. Her daughter lovingly confronted her, "Mom, you're bitter. Something's eating away at you. You've got to get rid of it ..." She opened her Bible. Putting her arm around her mother she read from Ephesians 4:30–31: *"And do not grieve the Holy Spirit of God, with whom you were sealed for the day of redemption. Get rid of all bitterness, rage and anger, brawling and slander, along with every form of malice."* They turned to Hebrews 12:14–15 *"Make every effort to live in peace with all men and to be holy; without holiness no one will see the Lord. See to it that no one misses the grace of God and that no bitter root grows up to cause trouble and defile many."*

They hugged and cried together. That began some deep soul searching, Margaret prayed, "God, what should I do with the guilt that other's should have? What is this bitterness that I'm experiencing? This anger? Why am I feeling so strongly about what's happened? I've tried never to let the sun go down on my wrath . . . I believe in settling matters. Help me, Lord. I need understanding and direction. I'm puzzled." God spoke to her and showed her how she was hurting herself and those she loved most.

By this time two Canadian lawyers and two American copyright lawyers were anxious to take up the case. It was not easy but she relinquished the issue, concluding it would harm the cause of God's name around the world if it were seen that Christians were fighting over the poem. Her uncle told her just leave it with the Lord. "Go home, write your heart out, and call it 'Leave it There'. That's what she did and the peace of God came flooding in. Not long after she started to receive requests for consent to use her poem. Hallmark cards asked her for permission to use *Footprints* and for another poem she had written. She says she can now walk into any bookstore and there is no longer any bitterness jealousy or anger. When she needed Him most God carried her.

All forgiveness requires a choice and a cost. This is why it can be so hard. It is being willing to bear another person's sins and actions against us. It is substitutional and is what Jesus did for us on the cross. When we forgive we bring to bear the power of the cross and we release grace. When we do not forgive we experience the power of what has been done against us and allow it to become part of us. Our heart becomes the incubator that breeds and nourishes the spiritual bacteria that have invaded. However much you nurse your wrath, it will never get any better.

The cycle of pain continues not only in us, but also through us. The word "resentment" literally means "to feel again" – it traps you to the past and in an endless cycle that keeps reliving what has been done to you. It picks at each fresh scab so that the wound is never allowed to heal. Every unhealed wound is a target for the enemy. The Apostle Paul warns us "letting the sun go down on your wrath" gives the devil a foothold, a legal entry point into our lives. He warned the church at Corinth not to withhold forgiveness otherwise the devil would gain an advantage over them (2 Corinthians 2:10–11).

The Greek word for "forgiveness" is *alphemi*, which means "to send away". It protects and guards the heart by searching to expel what has been done against us. If we don't forgive we become like those who have sinned against us. This is what led one immigrant Rabbi to say, "Before coming to America, I had to forgive Adolf Hitler. I did not want to bring Hitler inside me to my new country."[3]

At the end of the Lord's Prayer Jesus adds the strong warning:

> *"For if you forgive men when they sin against you, your heavenly Father will also forgive you. But if you do not forgive men their sins, your Father will not forgive your sins."* (Matthew 6:14–15)

He is not saying if you refuse to forgive someone you will lose your salvation and go to hell. He is stating that unforgiveness creates an attitude and a spirit which hinders the flow of God's grace and mercy to us.

In commenting on the beatitude *"Blessed are the merciful, for they will be shown mercy"* (Matthew 5:7), Selwyn Hughes the writer of *Every Day with Jesus* shares the following insight:

> "We must be careful here, for no beatitude has been more misunderstood than this one. There are those who take the words to mean that we can only be forgiven by God to the extent that we forgive others. They bring alongside this beatitude such passages as, *'Forgive us our sins, for we also forgive everyone who sins against us'* (Luke 11:4), and *'This is how my heavenly Father will treat each of you unless you forgive your brother from your heart'* (Matthew 18:35). Putting all these Scriptures together they claim that it is the clear meaning of the Bible that we are forgiven by God only to the degree that we forgive others. If this is so, then salvation is by works and not by grace. We must never interpret Scripture in a way that contradicts other Scriptures. What our Lord means in this beatitude is that when we demonstrate mercy to others, we make it possible for God's mercy to penetrate deeper into our own lives and personalities. The act of giving makes us more able to receive."[4]

Jesus says in Luke 6:36–38:

> *"Be merciful, just as your Father is merciful. 'Do not judge, and you will not be judged. Do not condemn, and you will not be condemned. Forgive, and you will be forgiven. Give, and it will be given to you. A good measure, pressed down, shaken together and running over, will be poured into your lap. For with the measure you use, it will be measured to you."*

This passage is frequently used to refer to financial giving but note its context is about forgiveness and judgment. Whatever we sow we will reap. If we want to go on experiencing mercy and forgiveness then we must keep on showing it.

Jesus told a parable that perfectly illustrates this. In Matthew 18 Peter comes and asks Jesus how often he should forgive. The Rabbi's had a saying, "If a man transgresses once forgive him, if a second time forgive him, if a third time forgive him, if a fourth time do not forgive him." So when Peter asks, "Should I forgive seven times?" he must have thought he was showing exceptional mercy. Jesus says not seven times but seventy times seven. In others words there should be no limit. He went on to tell a story about a man who begged for mercy and was forgiven a huge debt, he owed 10,000 talents. At that time the annual taxation of the provinces of Judea, Idumea, Samaria, Galilee and Perea was only 800 talents of gold. The point is the debt was unpayable, but he was forgiven. Yet this very person went and found someone who owed him in comparison only a few pounds and had him thrown in prison until he paid up. When the king heard about it he summoned the man who had such a huge debt cancelled and rebuked him saying he too should have had mercy on his debtors and had him thrown in jail and handed over to the tormentors. Jesus added, *"This is how my heavenly Father will treat each of you unless you forgive your brother from your heart"* (Matthew 18:35).

Note the emphasis on the heart because true, real forgiveness is a heart issue. It involves the mind and the will but fundamentally you can say you forgive through gritted teeth and acknowledge it in your head, but until it gets down into your heart you will always be held captive by what happened. The heart is where the pain is felt and it's the place from which pardon needs to flow.

If forgiveness doesn't visit the emotional core of past hurt our present healing will be incomplete. When the pain comes to the surface don't push it back down, allow the blood of Jesus and the power of the Holy Spirit to heal and redeem it.

When it's hard to forgive

Betrayed, rejected, slandered, abused, attacked, the list goes on and I am sure somewhere you have your own personal category that has affected you. It can be even harder to forgive when something has been done not against yourself, but someone you love. Sometimes we make forgiveness sound too light and simple. I know from many years of counseling and ministering to people who have been deeply wounded that healing and freedom only happens as they learn to forgive. I also know that sometimes to forgive is unbelievably hard.

Henri Nouwen wrote:

> "We've all been wounded. Who wounds us? Those we love and those who love us. When we feel rejected, abandoned, abused, manipulated or violated, it's usually by people close to us: our parents, our friends, our marriage partners, our children, our teachers, our pastors. This is what makes forgiveness so difficult. It's our hearts that are wounded! We cry out, 'You, who I expected to be there for me, have failed me. How can I ever forgive you for that?'"

Forgiveness is at the heart of the Gospel, but so is justice. This is very important for victims to understand. To forgive does not mean that what the person did against you does not matter and they just get away with it or you should let them do it again. It is recognizing that God is their judge and they will answer to Him. You are releasing them out of your judgment and into God's.

We need to be honest before God and tell Him how we feel. We also need to be honest with ourselves. The normal response to hurt is pain and anger, which are signs of healthy emotions. The Bible says, *"be angry and sin not"*. Don't become condemned for feeling the pain. Pain is saying you have been wounded and you had better do something about it or it will cripple you.

Corrie ten Boom was a remarkable woman who had an amazing ministry around the world but we would probably never have heard of her if she hadn't learnt to forgive. She was imprisoned with her sister Betsie by the Nazis for giving shelter to Jews during WW2. She spent several months in concentration camps but was miraculously released by an administrative error just before all the women in her unit were executed. She suffered many atrocities and the death of her beloved sister at the hands of the cruel guards. But by God's grace she learnt how to forgive. She wrote a little leaflet telling of one of the most dramatic moments of forgiveness, she called it, *I'm Still Learning to Forgive*.

> "It was in a church in Munich where I was speaking in 1947 that I saw him – a balding heavyset man in a gray overcoat, a

brown felt hat clutched between his hands. One moment I saw the overcoat and brown hat, the next, a blue uniform and a visored cap with its skull and crossbones. Memories of the concentration camp came back with a rush: the huge room with its harsh overhead lights, the pathetic pile of dresses and shoes in the centre of the floor, the shame of walking naked past this man. I could see my sister's frail form ahead of me, ribs sharp beneath the parchment of skin.

Betsie and I had been arrested for concealing Jews in our home during the Nazi occupation of Holland. This man had been a guard at Ravensbruck concentration camp where we were sent. Now he was in front of me, hand thrust out. 'A fine message, fraulein! How good it is to know that, as you say, all our sins are at the bottom of the sea!'

It was the first time since my release that I had been face to face with one of my captors and my blood seemed to freeze.

'You mentioned Ravensbruck in your talk,' he was saying, 'I was a guard there. But since that time,' he went on, 'I have become a Christian. I know that God has forgiven me for the cruel things I did there, but I would like to hear it from your lips as well. Fraulein.' Again the hand came out. 'Will you forgive me?'

And I stood there – I whose sins had again and again to be forgiven – and could not. Betsie had died in that place – could he erase her slow terrible death simply for the asking?

It could not have been many seconds that he stood there, hand held out, but to me it seemed hours as I wrestled with the most difficult thing I have ever had to do. For I had to do it – I knew that. The message that God forgives has a prior condition: that we forgive those who have injured us. 'If you do not forgive men their trespasses,' Jesus says, 'neither will your Father in Heaven forgive your trespasses.'

Still I stood there with the coldness clutching my heart. But forgiveness is an act of the will, and the will can function regardless of the temperature of the heart. 'Jesus help me!' I prayed silently. 'I can lift my hand. I can do that much. You supply the feeling.'

And so woodenly, mechanically, I thrust my hand into the one stretched out to me. And as I did, an incredible thing took place. The current started in my shoulder, raced down my arm, sprang into our joined hands. And then this healing warmth seemed to flood my whole being, bringing tears to my eyes. 'I forgive you brother!' I cried. 'With all my heart.'

For a long moment we grasped each other's hands, the former guard and former prisoner. I had never known God's love so intensely as I did then. But even so, I realised it was not my love. I had tried, and did not have the power. It was the power of the Holy Spirit as recorded in Romans 5:5, '... because the love of God is shed abroad in our hearts by the Holy Spirit which is given to us.'"[5]

Forgiving yourself

This can be even harder than forgiving others. In his book, *Spiritual Depression – Its Causes and Its Cure*, Dr Martyn Lloyd-Jones has a particularly relevant chapter called "That One Sin". He describes how, in his many years of pastoral experience, he frequently had to minister to people who were depressed because they were haunted by "that one sin".

> "In my experience of ministry, extending over many years, there is no more common difficulty. It is constantly recurring and I think that I have had to deal with more people over this particular thing than over anything else ... They could accept forgiveness for all kinds of transgressions, but always 'that one sin' kept coming back to haunt and depress them."[6]

He describes the case of an anguished man who, at the age of seventy-seven, escaped from living a completely godless life to the exuberant joy of becoming a Christian. It was he says, "One of the most striking conversions I have ever known." When he was accepted into membership and received his first communion, he was ecstatic. But the next morning he showed up, weeping uncontrollably. That one "self-rising" sin had come back to haunt him. He could accept that he was forgiven for the drinking and the gambling and immorality, but there was "that one sin". In a tavern, drinking and arguing religion, he had called Jesus illegitimate, using the crude 'B' word. That one sin he was sure, could never be forgiven. Lloyd-Jones was eventually able to convince him that Christ died and rose again for the forgiveness of all sins, including that one sin. His joy was restored.[7]

The real problem is not about being able to forgive yourself it is being unable to receive God's forgiveness into that area of your life. As long as we focus on ourselves and what we have done, we will never be free of it. One man, who was greatly disturbed about his sin wrote to Martin Luther. The great Reformer, who had agonized over his own shortcomings replied, "Learn to know Christ and Him crucified. Learn to sing to Him and say, Lord Jesus, You are my righteousness. You took on You what was mine; You set on me what was Yours. You became what You were not that I might become what I was not."

In Colossians chapter 2 the Apostle Paul tells us what God has done with our sin:

> *"When you were dead in your sins and in the uncircumcision of your sinful nature, God made you alive with Christ. He forgave us all our sins, having cancelled the written code, with its regulations, that was against us and stood opposed to us; he took it away, nailing it to the cross."*   (Colossians 2:13–14)

There are two Greek words he could have used for the word "cancelled". *Chiazesthai* means to cancel by writing an "X" across something. What's underneath is still seen but the "X" signifies that the debt is paid. Paul did not use this word, he used the word *exalpeinein*. The substance on which ancient documents were written was either papyrus, a kind of paper, or vellum, skins of animals. Both were very expensive and would not be wasted. Ancient ink had no acid, it did not bite the paper so to save the material a sponge was used and wiped out the handwriting as if it had never been there, with absolutely no trace left. In the New Covenant God cancels sin not by covering it but through cleansing it completely away. *"I will ... remember their sins no more"* (Hebrews 8:12).

There is no trace left.

Chapter 9

Righteousness

The breastplate of righteousness covers the heart.

During the course of twenty-one years of marriage one of the things that I have had to work at is shopping with my wife. It seems that a woman is able to spend hours just looking and have a wonderful time. I came across a slight variation of Caesar's supposed famous words when he landed in Britain, they were no doubt uttered by his wife, "Veni, Vedi, Visa: I came, I saw, I did a little shopping."

Some shops I like more than others such as food and furniture stores. On one such outing while looking for a sofa I noticed a sign advertising stain protection on almost every one in the shop. It read, "Don't let a spill become a stain." This miracle solution called "Scotch Guard" placed a protective coating over the material and kept it safe from all the messes and mistakes of life that would otherwise ruin it. The following Sunday morning guess what my sermon was titled? "Don't let a spill become a stain." Shopping can sometimes be inspirational after all.

One of the most important ways we guard our hearts is by learning to deal with the messes and mistakes of life quickly. When we have sinned or been sinned against don't let a spill sink into your heart and stain it. I am so thankful that the Bible doesn't say, "We reap what we sin", but rather, "We reap what we sow".

The Apostle John tells us that overcoming the world and walking in fellowship with God and each other is dependent on learning how to deal with sin (1 John). He says that if we walk in the light we have fellowship with God and one another and Jesus' blood will cleanse us from all unrighteousness. The meaning of the Greek word translated "cleanse" or "purify" implies a continuous action of washing and cleansing. It's not that we will never sin but we have such a desire for righteousness we walk in the light and immediately we spill or something is spilled over us we deal with it quickly. One of the most revealing tests of a person's spirituality is the time it takes them to deal with their sin.

Sin is always looking for a way in and follows the path of least resistance. God warned Cain:

> *"Why are you angry? Why is your face downcast? If you do what is right, will you not be accepted? But if you do not do what is right, sin is crouching at your door; it desires to have you, but you must master it."*   (Genesis 4:6–7)

Cain opened the door and in came the murder of his brother Abel. Sin looks for a way in to you to become a part of you. Then you sin not only from the temptation without but because of the desire within. It is not just something you do but is what you have become. You don't just tell a lie now and then, you have become a liar. You don't only steal when there is an opportunity, you look for things to steal because you have become a thief.

In the Sermon on the Mount Jesus said many words of comfort but He also gave some strong warnings. Speaking about sexual sin He taught that anyone who looks at a woman lustfully has already committed adultery with her in his heart. He is not saying that the person who has a fleeting immoral thought towards someone is the same as an adulterer but you could be on the way there unless you learn to deal with such thoughts quickly. We live in a fallen world and the images of sexual desire and fantasy are all around us and there are some things we can't help seeing. Jesus is not talking about this. He is referring not to a chance glance but a steady, longing, lustful gaze. We may not be responsible for the first sight but we always are when we choose to take a second and a third and a fourth. When you look lustfully it comes from within and impure thoughts are driving and seeking to dominate you. It's very revealing what we are told regarding King David and his adultery with Bathsheba, *"... he saw a woman bathing; and she was very lovely to behold"* (2 Samuel 11:2, Amplified Version). Martin Luther used to say, "A man might not be able to prevent a bird from flying over his head but he can stop it from nesting in his hair."

Talking about nests did you know that a cuckoo never builds a nest of its own? When it's due to lay an egg it finds another nest with eggs and no parent bird. The cuckoo lands hurriedly lays its egg, and takes off again. That's all the cuckoo does in terms of parenting. The thrush, whose nest has now been invaded, comes back, circles, and comes into the wind to land. Not being very good at arithmetic, it doesn't notice there are five eggs instead of four. It gets to work hatching the eggs. Four little thrushes and one large cuckoo eventually hatch. The cuckoo is two or three times the size of the others.

Mrs Thrush, having hatched the five little birds, goes off early in the morning to get the worm. She comes back, circles the nest to see four petite thrush mouths and one cavernous cuckoo mouth. Who gets the worm? The cuckoo, who gets bigger and bigger while the little thrushes get smaller and smaller. To find a baby cuckoo in a nest, simply walk along a hedgerow until you find little dead thrushes. The cuckoo throws them out one at a time. Finally the cuckoo takes over complete control. The moral to this injustice of nature, "Be very careful what you let into your nest [heart] or you will end up feeding that which will destroy you and those you love."

Understanding righteousness

In the oldest book of the Bible, Job asks the question, *"But how can a mortal be righteous before God?"* (Job 9:2). Righteousness is to be in right standing with a Holy God. It means that we measure up to His standards and they are absolute perfection. No wonder Job asks the question. Paul responds by telling us, *"For all have sinned and fall short of the glory of God"* (Romans 3:23) and *"There is no one righteous, not even one"* (Romans 3:10).

On the Jewish Day of Atonement the first sacrifice was not for the sins of the people but for the sins of the High Priest himself. He washed his hands and his feet, put off his gorgeous robes; clothed himself in spotless white linen. There was brought to him a bullock, which he had purchased with his own money. He laid both hands on the bullock's head to transfer his sin to it; and then made confession, "Ah, Lord God, I have committed iniquity; I have transgressed; I have sinned, I and my house. O Lord I beseech you, cover over the sins and transgressions which I have committed, transgressed and sinned before you, I and my house."

We all have a natural bias toward sin. You don't have to teach a child to be naughty and tell lies. It comes naturally. The

Scottish poet Robbie Burns stated this when he wrote, "My ancient but ignoble blood has crept through scoundrels since the flood." An unbeliever once told the Welsh evangelist Seth Joshua, "I can't swallow this doctrine of original sin." Joshua replied, "You don't have to it's inside you already." [1]

Guess when these were written:

> "I see no hope for the future of our people if they are dependent on the frivolous youth of today, for certainly all youth are reckless beyond words ... When I was young we were taught to be discreet and respectful of elders, but the present youth are exceedingly impatient of restraint."
>
> (Hesiod, Greek poet, eighth-century BC)

> "The children love luxury; they show disrespect for elders and love chatter in the place of exercise. Children are tyrants, not the servants of their households. They no longer rise when their elders enter the room. They contradict their parents, chatter before company, gobble up dainties at the table, cross their legs and tyrannise their teachers." [2]
>
> (Socrates, 469–399 BC)

One of my favorite stories is about a man in a supermarket pushing a trolley that contained not only two weeks' groceries but also a two-year-old child. The child was screaming, yelling and kicking but his father was speaking in soft measured tones. "Don't get upset George. Don't cry George. Don't scream George." An old lady nearby felt she must comment on this stunning example of fatherhood. "Sir," she said, "May I commend you on the way you are dealing with George." "Madam," he replied, "I'm George."

Sin is the same in all colors, cultures and countries. Interestingly enough, wherever you go in the world occultism is also the same because the root of all occult powers flows from the same demonic fountain. Kurt Koch, a German theologian and recognised authority, has investigated, lectured and ministered extensively on healing and deliverance from demonic powers. He observed,

> "As a part of folklore occultism has been practiced for thousands of years. There are two main features characteristic of all the material I have been able to collect on this

subject from the 120 or so countries I have visited during 40 years of ministry.

Firstly, historically speaking the rules of occultism have remained unchanged throughout all the different epochs of man. The actual practices of occultism are the same today as they were 5000 years ago.

Secondly, no matter what the level of civilisation, the methods used by that civilisation remain the same. The form may change but the underlying principles remain the same. This similarity puzzles ethnologists, anthropologists and psychologists a great deal."[3]

The power of the Gospel is also the same in all nations. One of the great joys of traveling is to meet people who by birth and culture could not be more different than you and yet you know immediately there is a common bond between you. The work of the Holy Spirit in their life is the same as in your own. The Jesus you love they love. The power of the blood of Jesus that set you free set them free. The same righteousness of Christ that saved you saved them.

This is the same throughout history. We sing hymns written hundreds of years ago by men like Charles Wesley and know exactly what he meant when he wrote, "My chains fell off my heart was free, I rose went forth and followed Thee". Or John Newton's "Amazing Grace" and Isaac Watts' "When I survey the wondrous cross". Two of my favorite hymns are "Jesus the very thought of Thee" written by Bernard of Clairvaux and "Be thou my vision O Lord of my heart" both over a thousand years old.

Luther and righteousness

It is God's righteousness that condemns us because of our sin, but it is also His righteousness that saves us when we receive Jesus as our Lord and Savior. It was this revelation that led to the conversion of Martin Luther and the Reformation that followed.

Luther became an Augustinian monk and did all he could to make himself right with God. He fasted, beat his body, punished himself, prayed, and went on pilgrimages but felt totally miserable, lost and condemned.

His tutor Von Staupitz encouraged him to study the Psalms as a place to find comfort and peace. As Luther read Psalm 31 the verse *"Deliver me in Thy Righteousness"* began to pour light and hope into his soul. Then he studied the book of Romans and there in chapter 1:17 he read again about "The righteousness of God". He describes his experience when at last he understood what it meant:

> "I greatly longed to understand Paul's epistle to the Romans and nothing stood in my way but that one expression, 'The Righteousness of God' because I took it to mean that righteousness whereby God is righteous and deals righteously punishing the unrighteous ... Night and day I pondered until I saw the connection between the righteousness of God and the statement that 'The just shall live by faith'.
>
> Then I grasped that the righteousness of God is that righteousness by which through grace and sheer mercy God justifies us through faith. Hereupon I felt myself to be reborn and to have gone through open doors into paradise.
>
> The whole of scripture took on a new meaning and whereas before the Righteousness of God had filled me with hate, now it became to me inexpressibly sweet in greater love. This passage in Paul became a gateway to heaven."[4]

The throne of Judgment becomes a throne of grace when we come before it in the righteousness of Christ through His shed blood, the Lamb slain before it.

Fifteen hundred years before Luther the Apostle Paul had the same experience. He tells us about it in the book of Philippians chapter 3, where he presents his religious CV and says it was like human refuse so far as being able to make him right before God. It was the righteousness that comes only from and through Christ that he prized, and compared with that all his past accomplishments were like so much garbage. He came to understand that it wasn't only his bad deeds that had kept him from God it was also trusting in his good works and own righteousness. It's the same with those who when you ask them why they should be allowed into heaven and answer, "I try and live a good life," "I give to charity," "I try and do the best I can." All these are good but they are trusting in themselves. It's not only bad things we have done that block the way to heaven, it is also trusting in the good we do. No one can enter without the righteousness of Jesus.

Imputed and imparted

God's righteousness is both imputed and imparted. What exactly does this mean?

When someone accepts Jesus as their Lord and Savior, Jesus' righteousness is imputed or credited to them. He becomes their righteousness that makes them right with God.

> *"God made him who had no sin to be sin for us, so that in him we might become the righteousness of God."*
>
> (2 Corinthians 5:21)

Our name has been transferred to the Lamb's book of life and His record is now accredited to us. In this sense we are saved by works, but not our works. We are forgiven because of what Christ has done for us. We need to note also that it is not even our faith that saves us. If it were, then we would be turning faith into a work. We are saved by God's grace through faith:

> *"For it is by grace you have been saved, through faith – and this not from yourselves, it is the gift of God."*   (Ephesians 2:8)

God's grace is the source and faith is the channel.

This righteousness is imputed and declares us perfect in God's sight. It does not mean that we are already perfected. Just ask my wife. Ask your wife or husband or honest friend. We still have all kinds of faults and failings. An acorn has within it a perfect oak tree, but it is still just an acorn. When it is planted and nourished it grows into a full-grown tree – now it has become perfected. It is God's imparted righteousness that perfects us. It sets us free from sinful habits and character traits establishing His reign within us. He does this as we co-operate with the Holy Spirit and we are changed more and more into the likeness of Jesus.

In his book *Lectures to My Students* Charles Haddon Spurgeon begins with these inspiring and challenging words:

> "Every workman knows the necessity of keeping his tools in a good state of repair. If the workman loses the edge he knows that there will be a greater draw upon his energy, or his work will be badly done. It will be vain for me to stock my library, or organise societies, or project schemes, if I neglect the culture of myself: for books and agencies and

systems are only remotely the instruments of my holy calling. My own spirit, soul and body are my nearest machinery for sacred service, my spiritual faculties and my inner life are my battleaxe and weapons for war!!

Then quoting from a letter of the great Scottish minister, Robert Murray M'Cheyne, he concludes:

"Do not forget the culture of the inner man – I mean of the heart. Remember you are God's Sword, instrument, I trust a chosen vessel unto Him to bear His Name. In great measure according to the purity and perfection of the instrument will be the success. It is not great talent God blesses so much as likeness to Jesus. A Holy minister is an awful weapon in the hands of God." [5]

A Roman soldier was trained to aim for either the head or the heart as this was the quickest way to disable and kill an opponent. This is why the Apostle Paul in writing about spiritual warfare tells us to put on the *"helmet of salvation"* and the *"breastplate of righteousness"*, which are Christ's imputed and imparted righteousness.

Chapter 10

The Power of a Thankful Heart

Pain is inevitable misery is optional.

Richard Wurmbrand was imprisoned several times by the Nazis for his faith, and spent a further fourteen years in jail in communist Romania. For three years he was alone in a cell thirty feet below ground, never seeing sun, moon or stars or another man's face except for the guards and interrogators who beat and tortured him. His book *Tortured for Christ* not only opened the eyes of the West to what Christians were suffering in communist captivity but also to the extraordinary character and ministry of this man and others like him.

In another of his books, *Sermons in Solitary Confinement*, telling of this time he says he rarely slept at night but only during the day. He passed the night hours in prayer and composing sermons. One of these midnight messages he calls "Gagged Again".

"Again there have been the yelling cries, which neither I nor the other prisoners can master. I am in a strait-jacket and gagged for the second time . . . I wonder how St. Francis of Assisi would have felt in my place. I remember his conversation with Brother Leo, who asked him wherein is perfect joy? Does it lie in knowing many things? Francis denied this. Is it in being a prophet and knowing the mysteries of God? Francis shook his head. Leo asked, is it in winning many souls for Christ. The answer was the same, no. Was it then in great sanctity and performing miracles for the good of men? Francis answered; 'None of these things can give perfect joy . . . we shall know perfect joy if we remain hungry and outside the walls of the monastery, enduring the rain and the mud with gladness and patience and thankfulness. The cross is the only tree on which the flower of perfect joy will grow.' [Wurmbrand added]: I have the cross. So I decided to be joyful, and I danced."[1]

During his imprisonment he asked a fellow prisoner he had led to the Lord before they were arrested, "Have you any resentment against me that I brought you to Christ?" The man replied, "I have no words to express my thankfulness that you brought me to this wonderful Saviour. I would never have it any other way."

The devil will never be able to defeat the power of a heart thankful to God.

When John Wesley was about twenty-one years of age he went to study at Oxford University. He came from a Christian home, and he was gifted with a keen mind and good looks. Yet in those days he was a bit snobbish and sarcastic. One night, however, something happened that set in motion a change in his heart. While speaking with a porter, he discovered that the poor fellow had only one coat and lived in such impoverished conditions that he didn't even have a bed. Yet he was an unusually happy person, filled with gratitude to God. Wesley, being immature, thoughtlessly joked about the man's misfortunes. "And what else do you thank God for?" he said with a touch of sarcasm. The porter smiled, and in the spirit of meekness replied with joy, "I thank Him that He has given me my life and being, a heart to love Him, and above all a constant desire to serve Him!"

Deeply moved, Wesley recognised that this man knew the meaning of true thankfulness and it was something he never forgot. When he lay on his deathbed those who gathered around him realised how well he had learned the lesson of praising God in every circumstance. Despite his extreme weakness, he gathered his strength and cried out, "The best of all is, God is with us," and then, he lifted up his arm in a token of victory and raised his feeble voice with a holy triumph and repeated, "The best of all is, God is with us!" Most of his last night on earth he was heard to repeat, "I'll praise – I'll praise."[2]

The quality of our lives is dependent on the quality of our thoughts and these are determined by the thankfulness of our hearts to God. The Apostle Paul understood this. Writing to the church at Philippi he thanks them for their kind gift and encourages them to continually rejoice and be joyful. Even though he is in chains his thankfulness to God pulsates throughout the whole book. At least nineteen times "joy" and "rejoice" are mentioned, and the mind and the way we are to think is referred to on fifteen occasions. Even more than this Jesus is spoken of almost forty times.

He tells the church:

> *"Rejoice in the Lord always. I will say it again: Rejoice! Let your gentleness be evident to all. The Lord is near. Do not be anxious about anything, but in everything, by prayer and petition, with thanksgiving, present your requests to God. And the peace of God, which transcends all understanding, will guard your hearts and your minds in Christ Jesus."* (Philippians 4:4–7)

Have you ever wondered why it is that some people have so much and yet never seem to be genuinely happy, while others with little have such joy? It is because real, life-tingling joy is about what's happening on the inside of you more than on the outside. A thankful heart to God creates the environment and the atmosphere that gives you the power to enjoy life.

Note the words *"with thanksgiving"* – this is because a thankful heart turns our focus to God and not ourselves or our problems. It's possible to spend hours in prayer and come away feeling worse and more fearful than when we began. This is because all we have done is recite our problems and worries and caused them to grow as we have focused on them instead of on God who is bigger and greater than whatever we are facing. A heart filled with thanksgiving sees God over and above all we are going through.

Paul tells us, *"the peace of God ... will guard* [our] *hearts and* [our] *minds"* the word "guard" literally means "to build a stockade around". It is what Roman soldiers erected around their camps to protect themselves from surprise and savage attacks of their enemies. God builds a stronghold of peace around our hearts and minds as we pray with thanksgiving.

Several years ago this truth became a lifesaver to me when I was extremely ill. I was fragile and vulnerable. When I prayed I often felt worse because all I was doing was focusing on my feelings and pain. My heart was heavy and overwhelmed. God spoke to me from this passage and I made sure that my prayers became filled with thanks. I made lists of all the things in my life to celebrate and thank God for. I made up songs and sang hymns filled with thanksgiving and praise. I thanked God for the measure of health and strength I had. I thanked Him for my salvation, my family, my friends, His promises, His faithfulness. An African proverb I had heard now became far more meaningful: "I complained I had no shoes until I met a man who had no feet." I had so many things in my life to be thankful for. There are times when we have to prime the pump of praise and make the "choice to rejoice". Our faith has to rise above our feelings and our will over our emotions.

I read a story of a young child who had only recently become a Christian who came down from her bedroom one morning and said to her mother, "What a beautiful day." Her surprised mum said, "What do you mean? It's raining torrents outside and the weather forecast is that it will last all week. How can you call such weather beautiful?" "But mother," the little girl replied, "A beautiful day has nothing to do with the weather." It's sad when our joy is at the mercy of whether it rains or not or what other people say or do. It's not what's going on around us but what's happening within us that makes us thankful people.

In everything and for everything

Whatever we are able to thank God in and for, loses its power to steal our joy and peace. Paul understood this when he wrote:

> *"Be joyful always; pray continually; give thanks in all circumstances, for this is God's will for you in Christ Jesus."*
> (1 Thessalonians 5:16–18)

> *" . . . Sing and make music in your heart to the Lord, always giving thanks to God the Father for everything, in the name of our Lord Jesus Christ."* (Ephesians 5:19–20)

In everything and for everything is about as absolute as you can get. It leaves nothing out. The moment I cease to have a thankful heart I have stepped outside God's will for my life and His provision for my well-being.

"In everything give thanks" doesn't cause us too many difficulties but it is Paul's teaching that we "give thanks for everything" that creates theological and practical problems. Does he mean that we must thank God for every tragedy and heartache that comes our way? The answer is yes and no. No, we don't thank Him for the evil and the suffering. No, we don't thank Him for the pain and the anguish of what is clearly the devil's work. But yes, we do thank Him that no matter what happens He is in ultimate control even in such a crazy fallen world. He knows what it is like to be abused, betrayed, reviled and have evil heaped upon Him. God the Father knows what it is to see a son suffer and die. We thank Him that He not only knows what we are going through, He understands. We thank Him that He is a faithful and just God and no one will ever escape His justice and righteous ways. We thank Him that He is able to bring healing and redeem even the worst that we experience. We give thanks because He is able to make all things work together for good.

The Greek word translated "for [everything]" is *huper*, which has the root meaning of "over and above". Paul is saying that we are to let our thanks rise over and above all that we are going through. This is the way to soar and rise above the circumstances instead of living under them, but it requires faith and discernment. It's not some robotic response that says I must give thanks because I am supposed to, yet deep down inside I am confused and hurting. We need wisdom to recognise evil and not blame God.

Matthew Henry the great Bible commentator, records in his diary a time when he was attacked by thieves and robbed of his purse. He wrote, "Let me be thankful, first because I was never robbed before. Secondly, they took my purse but they did not take my life. Thirdly, though they took my all it was not very much. Lastly, it was I who was robbed and not someone else." [3]

Thanks releases grace

Grace by its very nature cannot be earned or deserved. It is God's unmerited favor. Yet James tells us that *"God opposes the proud but gives grace to the humble"* (James 4:6). We can position ourselves to receive it through humility and thanksgiving.

In Hebrews 12:28 we read in the King James Authorised Version:

> *"Wherefore we receiving a kingdom, which cannot be moved, let us have grace, whereby we may serve God acceptably with reverence and godly fear."*

In the New International Version we read:

> *"Therefore, since we are receiving a kingdom that cannot be shaken, let us be thankful, and so worship God acceptably with reverence and awe."*

The AV says, *"Let us have grace"*; the NIV says, *"Let us be thankful"*. They are both correct because in the Greek language to have "grace" (*charis*) is to say, "Thank you". When we say grace at meal times we are "giving thanks". The late Bible teacher and author Derek Prince comments, "When we are unthankful we are out of the grace of God. We cannot enjoy God's grace without being thankful. Nor can we separate thankfulness from the grace of God, and whether we say, 'let us be thankful' or 'Let us have grace', we are really saying the same thing." [4]

The modern Greek word for "thank you" is *eucharisto*, which is directly related to grace. You may recognise a similar word "Eucharist" that is used of The Lord's Table. Paul speaks of the *"cup of thanksgiving"* (1 Corinthians 10:16). Jesus broke the bread saying, *"This is my body"*, and as He did so *"He gave thanks"*. After the meal Matthew tells us they followed the Passover custom of singing a hymn together. During the Passover they would have sung portions from Psalms 113–118 but now they would sing the "Great Hallel" that was Psalm 136. As Jesus prepared for what was to come in Gethsemane, the scourging, the betrayal and forsakenness of the cross, He lifted His voice, *"Give thanks to the* Lord, *for he is good. His love endures forever. Give thanks to the God of gods. His love endures forever. Give thanks to the Lord of lords: His love endures forever"* (Psalm 136:1–3).

There was another occasion when Jesus took bread and gave thanks. It was the feeding of the five thousand – the only miracle He did that is recorded in all four gospels. The Apostle John refers to that moment later in the same chapter, *"Then some boats from Tiberias landed near the place where the people had eaten the bread after the Lord had given thanks"* (John 6:23). He doesn't highlight the miracle but rather the place where Jesus had *"given thanks"*. It was this that released the grace to feed so many with so little.

C.S. Lewis observed:

> "We do not really receive something unless we give thanks for it. The very action of saying 'thank you' and meaning it, opens up the spirit to a true sense of appreciation. In giving thanks something moves inside the centre of our spirits and allows the wonder of what has been done for us to invade us." [5]

Chapter 11

The Word

*Either sin will keep you from this Book or
this Book will keep you from sin.*
(D.L. Moody speaking about the Bible)

In his book *A People Saturated with God*, Brian Edwards gives a
very revealing insight regarding the people God uses in revival
and their love for the word of God.

> "All who have been used by God in spiritual revival were
> diligent in the study of Scripture and the application of
> Scripture to their own lives. God uses men and women who
> submit to His authority. He does not begin revival with
> those who have no interest in His Word ... He will not trust
> revival to those who will not trust His Word. It has to be
> stated as a point of historical fact that revival never begins
> with the 'liberal' wing of the church, that is those who deny
> the full authority and accuracy of Scripture. I am not aware
> of any exception to this. Of course those who are critical of
> Scripture may subsequently be swept into revival and
> receive full blessing from it, but their attitude to the Word
> of God will change." [1]

One of the great declarations of the Reformation was *"Sola
Scriptura"* – Scripture alone. Not church councils and traditions
but what does God's Word say? Martin Luther declared, "My
conscience is captive to the Word of God." As a result a great
revival took place across Europe as the entrance of God's Word
brought light and life to those who were now coming out of both
the historical and spiritual Dark Ages.

Tragically, the same nation that gave us Luther and the Reformation also gave us two world wars. It was German theologians

who led the way in attacking the authority and trustworthiness of the Bible, and the resulting spiritual decline created a vacuum that gave rise to the likes of Adolf Hitler and the Nazi party with their occultic practices and beliefs. They were obsessed with astrology and the belief of the supremacy of the German Aryan people. These demonic convictions were behind their hatred and attack of the Christian church and the murder of over six million Jews.

The devil hates the Word of God because like no other book the Bible has the power not only to inform but also to transform a person's life. In his moving story, *Miracle on the River Kwai*, Ernest Gordon tells of his captivity as a Japanese prisoner of war among the men building the infamous Burma Railway. They were treated worse than animals and endured horrific conditions, with what seemed like no hope or purpose to life. Yet even here, God's Word brought about a remarkable transformation.

A few Christians reading their Bibles formed Bible study groups and as they shared and studied with others there came remarkable changes in the camp. Something wonderful began to happen in the hearts of POWs who had stolen from and cheated one another just to survive, as they became men who cared for and even gave their lives for each other. Those death camps became a place of hope and life because God's Word was at work.

Gordon recounts that during one work detail a shovel went missing. As the party was about to be dismissed, the Japanese guard shouted that a shovel was unaccounted for. He insisted that someone had stolen it. Striding up and down before the men he ranted and denounced them for their wickedness and, most unforgivable of all, their ingratitude to the Emperor. As he raved, he worked himself up into a paranoid fury. Screaming in broken English, he demanded that the guilty person step forward to take his punishment. No one moved; the guard's rage reached new heights of violence. "All die! All die!" he shrieked. To show that he meant what he said, he cocked his rifle, put it to his shoulder and looked down the gun sights, ready to fire at the first man at the end of them. At that moment one of the men stepped forward, stood stiffly to attention, and said calmly, "I did it." The guard unleashed all his whipped up hatred; he kicked the helpless prisoner and beat him with his fists. Seizing his rifle by the barrel, he lifted it high over his head and, with a final howl, brought it down on the soldier's skull. The soldier sank limply to the ground and did not move. The men of the work detail picked up their comrade's body, shouldered their tools and marched back to the camp. When the tools were counted again at the guardhouse no shovel was missing.[2]

At the end of the war, Gordon went to theological college in Edinburgh and then to Hartford Theological Seminary, Connecticut. He served as assistant minister at Paisley Abbey before returning to America to become Dean of the Chapel of Princeton University.

The Word of God has the power to set us free and keep us free. I will never forget the night that as a young Christian I knelt before God with tears streaming down by face. I wanted more than anything to serve Him but there was a recurring temptation that I was battling with. I cried out to God for help and in desperation I took hold of my Bible and opened it to read these life changing words that jumped out at me – words I didn't even know were there:

> *"How can a young man keep his way pure?*
> *By living according to your word.*
> *I seek you with all my heart;*
> *do not let me stray from your commands.*
> *I have hidden your word in my heart*
> *that I might not sin against you."* (Psalm 119:9–11)

That moment was one of the most joyful and victorious in my life.

God's Word strengthens and sustains us. It is a lamp to our feet and nourishment to our soul. It is a shield and fortress against the enemy. When Jesus was tempted in the wilderness, each time He responded to Satan's attack by quoting the Word of God. Job tells us what helped sustain him in his suffering:

> *"I have not departed from the commands of his lips;*
> *I have treasured the words of his mouth more than*
> *my daily bread."* (Job 23:12)

Jeremiah says the same about his trials:

> *"When your words came, I ate them;*
> *they were my joy and my heart's delight."* (Jeremiah 15:16)

The devil isn't too bothered by our words, theories and philosophies but he is terrified of the Word of God.

I came across an amusing story sometime ago, it was said to be true and it would be great if it were. An elderly lady had just returned home after church when she was startled to find an intruder robbing her home. She had heard her pastor teaching about the power of God's Word and yelled, "Stop! Acts 2:38!" (which reads, "turn from your sin."). The burglar stopped dead in his tracks as the woman calmly called the police and explained what she had done. When the officers arrived and handcuffed the man, they asked him why he had just stood there and waited for them, as all the old lady had done was yell a scripture at him. "Scripture" replied the thief, "She said she had an axe and two 38s."

How do we hide God's Word in our hearts?

Permit me to bore you for a few moments with some statistics about cricket (unless you are a cricket fan). England's highest score against Australia was 903 for 7 at the Oval in 1930. Len Hutton scored a then world test match record of 364 runs. The highest number of first-class centuries is 197 by Jack Hobbs. Donald Bradman's first-class average is 99.94. I could go on and on. I first read all these statistics as an eleven-year-old over thirty years ago, and they are still memorable to me today. I wasn't just reading about a sport I watched, but something I loved. What we learn goes into our heads and may or may not be remembered. But what we love goes into our hearts and becomes a part of who we are. Learning biblical texts is not the same as loving the truth of God's Word. When you love someone you will want to read their love letters to you. So don't just read God's Word, seed it into your heart by meditating on its truth and most of all by spending time with the author. Reading the Bible without meditating on it is like trying to eat without swallowing.

Search me

The heart not only requires a place for truth to come into, but an exit to get rid of the rubbish that gets dumped there. God's Word will expose these pollutants as we spend time in His presence. Psalm 139 is a love song of deepest intimacy between David and God. Intimacy simply means "into me see". David ends by asking,

"Search me, O God, and know my heart;
test me and know my anxious thoughts.
See if there is any offensive way in me,
and lead me in the way everlasting." (Psalm 139:23–24)

The word "search" means "to dig down deep". Our hearts can become cluttered and the problem with such mess is that it has the tendency to make itself almost invisible after it's been there for some time. This creates "blind spots" sins we have excused or rationalised that we no longer notice. David calls them *"hidden faults"* (Psalm 19:12). Ask a teenager about the mess in their room and they invariably answer "what mess?"

One preacher asked his congregation, "How many of you believe all you see on the television?" Not surprisingly no one did. He then asked, "How many of you believe all you hear on the radio?" Again nobody. "How many of you believe all you read in the newspapers?" Again no one. "How many of you believe the Bible to be the Word of God?" Everyone enthusiastically raised their hands. He said, "One last question, how many of you spend more time reading, watching and listening to what you don't believe than what you do believe?" Everyone got the point.

When we fill our hearts and minds with the world we shouldn't be surprised when we think and act as the world does. When we are more filled with doubt than faith, is it any wonder the devil is able to oppress and discourage us? Saving and miracle working faith come through a heart captured with God's Word.

"... if you confess with your mouth, 'Jesus is Lord,' and believe in your heart ... you will be saved." (Romans 10:9)

"I tell you the truth, if anyone says to this mountain, 'Go, throw yourself into the sea,' and does not doubt in his heart but believes that what he says will happen, it will be done for him."
(Mark 11:23)

When the Word becomes flesh miracles happen.

Chapter 12

Don't Lose Heart

You are never beaten until you are defeated on the inside.[1]

What do these people have in common – William Wilberforce, Abraham Lincoln, Mother Teresa, Gladys Aylwood, and William Carey? They all accomplished great things for God despite going through times of intense disappointment and discouragement. There are countless others for whom this is true, but let's have a look at these few.

Wilberforce

William Wilberforce will forever be associated with the abolition of the slave trade throughout the British Empire. He was the abolitionist's greatest champion. Speaking to Parliament, he said, "I confess to you, so enormous, so dreadful, so irremediable did its wickedness appear that my own mind was completely made up for abolition. Let the consequences be what they would, I from this time determine that I would never rest until I had effected its Abolition."

He was harassed by warnings from merchants and planters that it would ruin the West Indies and devastate the British Empire's economy. The alternatives, the trade or ruin, looked dreadful but he could not believe that God, however mysterious His ways, had so constituted the world that the prosperity of one part depended on the depopulation and devastation of another.

Contemplating the opposition, the possibility of physical assault and of losing friends, Wilberforce's faith in God sustained him as he prayed: "Almighty God under all my weakness and uncertain prospects give me grace to trust firmly in thee, that I may not sink under my sorrows nor disquieted with the scars of those evils which cannot without thy permission fall upon me."[2]

In the midst of the battle he received the encouragement of John Wesley from one of the last letters Wesley wrote, aged eighty-seven, the day before the onset of his brief final illness, "Unless God has raised you up for this very thing, you will be worn out by the opposition of men and devils. But if God be for you, who can be against you."[3]

It was a long hard struggle with so many prejudices and vested interests to be overcome that it took forty-five years of his life to see the Bill abolishing the slave trade and then slavery throughout the British Empire passed. It came before Parliament and was rejected many times: 1789, 1791, 1792, 1793, 1794, 1795, 1796, 1797, 1798, 1804, 1805 and 1806. On 25 March, 1807, the Bill for the Abolition of the Slave Trade finally became law. This was not the end of the battle as the problems of enforcing it throughout the Empire would not be easy. What was needed was the abolition of not just the slave trade but the abolition of slavery and for this Wilberforce now gave his all. It was to come twenty-six years later when he was on his deathbed that he finally heard, late on Friday, 26 July, 1833, that the Abolition of Slavery Bill had been passed by Parliament. Slavery as a legal state was now to all intents dead in the British Empire. "Thank God," said Wilberforce, "that I have lived to witness a day in which England is willing to give twenty millions sterling for the Abolition of Slavery."[4] Three days later on 29 July he passed into the presence of his Lord.

Lincoln

Abraham Lincoln was arguably America's greatest president and one of this world's great leaders. He was an agnostic until he reached the age of forty, then he read Dr James Smith's brilliant examination called *The Christian's Defence*, which proved the historical reality of the events of Christ's life. The overwhelming evidence from this book convinced Lincoln with the result that he became a genuine Christian for the rest of his life. He says, "My doubts scattered to the winds and my reason became convinced by the arguments in support of the inspired and infallible authority of the Old and New Testaments."

His early life was filled with failure and setbacks. He failed in his first attempt at business. He then tried politics and within only one year failed there also. He went back to business for yet another try and failed again. Three failures in three years. He asked his fiancée to marry him after four years of courtship, but she said no. Later, another sweetheart died. He struggled for the next two years and suffered a nervous breakdown. After taking two years to recover, he tried once again in the political world and was defeated in his bid to be elected as Speaker of the House.

Two years later he sought to be appointed as the Elector and was again defeated. Three years after this he ran for a seat in Congress and was defeated. He waited another five years to run for office again, and was defeated. It was during this time that his four-year-old son died. He spent the next seven years in relative obscurity and then ran yet again for a political office, this time in the Senate. Again he was defeated. The following year, he was nominated by his party to be the candidate for Vice-President, but was defeated along with his running mate. After two more years he tried again for the Senate seat, but was defeated. Two years later, in 1860, Abraham Lincoln was elected as the 16th President of the United States.[5]

Even then he was derided and was one of the most slandered presidents in American history. Slave owners and politicians alike hated him. Newspapers branded him a grotesque baboon, a third-rate country lawyer who once split rails and now splits the union. In the Illinois Register he was labelled, "The most dishonest politician that ever disgraced an office." The *Chicago Times* called the Gettysburg Address "Shameful. A silly flat dish watery utterance and an embarrassment to the country." History has shown him to be a man of integrity and greatness who led the fight for the abolition of slavery in America and was able to hold that nation together after a terrible civil war.

These principles for truth and liberty finally cost him his life. In his book, *A Temple of Topaz* F.W. Boreham writes about Lincoln's life and death. He says of that last fateful night at Ford's Theatre in Washington:

> "Lincoln leaned forward, talking under his breath, to Mrs. Lincoln. Now that the war is over, he said he would take her for a tour of the East. They would visit Palestine and see Gethsemane and Calvary and would walk together the streets of Jeru ... !"

But before the word was finished a pistol shot, "the maddest pistol shot in the history of the ages" rang through the theatre. And he turned his pilgrim feet towards the holiest heights of all."

Mother Teresa

A Nobel Prize winner and a remarkable woman who at the age of eighteen entered a religious order that sent her to Calcutta, India where she took the name Sister Teresa. For the next ten years she worked in a school connected to the convent but all the while the desperate poverty in the streets of Calcutta haunted her. The Holy Spirit was calling to her through the poor but what could she do? She was a slight woman and her health was threatened by tuberculosis. And yet again and again she heard a voice calling her, insisting she must do something.

In the summer of 1946 she went by train to Darjeeling to make her annual retreat. All the way she was obsessed with images she had seen on Calcutta's streets, stinking slums, dying children, dogs eating living foetuses, a little boy whose mother had tried to strangle him. At last she surrendered to God's call. She would leave her order and devote herself entirely to the poor. Although she faced opposition from her superiors eventually she received permission to leave the convent. After taking a three-month course from an order of medical sisters she sought out Calcutta's most miserable slums. She went from hut to hut washing and feeding all the children she could find. After three days she started an open-air school.

She began to look for homeless people who were too weak to move, their bodies stretched out on the pavements lying so still she could barely tell the dead from the living. The first woman she took off the street was half eaten by rats and ants; another old woman had been thrown out with the garbage by her son. Teresa took them to the hospital and insisted that they be given medical care.

Each day she worked all alone and became exhausted and discouraged and the temptation to return to her order grew stronger. Yet still she insisted to herself, "The Lord wants me where I am – He will provide the answers."

The then Archbishop of Calcutta, Henry D'Souza, said that at times in her life, Mother Teresa battled terrible discouragement. He said that in one letter, she wrote she had been walking the streets of Calcutta searching for a house where she could start her work. At the end of the day, she wrote in her diary, "I wandered the streets the whole day. My feet are aching, and I have not been able to find a home. I also get the Tempter telling me, 'Leave all this, go back to the convent from which you came.'"[6]

Just when she thought she could hold out no longer, the Lord did provide. A government official gave her a room to use and support began to pour in from teachers, students and mothers of families. In 1950 she founded a new order "The Missionary Sisters of Charity" to care for the poor and homeless and dying. Today the order she established "The Missionaries of Charity" feed 500,000 families, treats 90,000 leprosy patients and educates 20,000 children in Calcutta alone every year.

Gladys Aylwood

Anyone who has seen the film, *The Inn of the Sixth Happiness* will know immediately the woman I am talking about. No, not Ingrid Bergman but the person she portrayed, Gladys Aylwood. She was rejected by the China Missionary Society as someone with no experience, or the expertise necessary to go as a missionary to China, but God opened the doors for her to go.

When the Japanese invaded she was forced to flee when they threatened the province of Yong Cheng where she had a mission station. With only one assistant she led more than a hundred orphans over the mountains to safety. During the journey she said she grappled with despair as never before. After passing a sleepless night she faced the morning with no hope of reaching safety. A thirteen-year-old girl in the group reminded her of their much-loved story of Moses crossing the Red Sea. "But I am not Moses" she cried in desperation. "Of course you aren't," the girl said, "but Jehovah is still God." They made it through and she did amazing work for God in that land.

Know who is against you and who is for you

An old Chinese proverb says, "Know your enemy then in 100 battles you will be victorious 100 times." There is an imaginary story told of how one day the devil called all his demons and chief lieutenants together and laid out a variety of viscious weapons on a table. They were invited to choose and use any that they wished in an assault upon the Christian church. Each weapon carried both a price tag and a label. One was designated anger, others lust, bitterness, envy etc. There was a weapon there, however, that stood out from all the rest. The label was turned over. The devil was asked what this awful instrument was. He replied that it was his very own possession. It was the one that made entry possible for all the others. When the tag was turned over the letters spelt out the word "discouragement".

Elijah battled with this as he sat down underneath a juniper tree and wanted to die. He was an outstanding prophet of God who only hours previously had prayed down fire on Mount Carmel and a rainstorm on a drought stricken nation. He had comprehensively defeated the false prophets of Baal and Ashtoreth and conducted his most powerful and successful crusade meeting to date. He was expecting this to precipitate a great spiritual revival with national repentance and the people returning to God. There were some signs of such a stirring but it appears to have been short lived. Jezebel, King Ahab's wife, went into a rage when she heard what had happened and lifted up her voice against Elijah and filled him and most of the nation with fear and intimidation. If Elijah ran away how could others stand up to this demonically inspired queen?

Elijah was physically, emotionally and spiritually exhausted. He felt a failure and told God that he was no better than his forefathers. It seemed to him the last several years of battling against a godless king and devilish queen had been a waste of time. His morale had never been so low. He hung his head as his heart was filled with despair. He'd had enough. He was totally discouraged and wanted to die.

Ever been there? Is there a way back or are such times really the end? These moments are not the time for making major decisions. Elijah was confused. He was running to save his life but all he wanted to do was die. When you are this discouraged you become unsure about everything. When God spoke to him at Mount Horeb Elijah said that he was the only one left who hadn't bowed the knee to foreign gods, but Obadiah had already told him he had hidden a hundred of the Lord's prophets safely in a cave and he himself was a devout believer in the Lord. Discouragement is a disconcerting and lonely place. Elijah's dream had been revival and now this hope that hadn't materialized the way he expected began to make his heart feel sick.

To be restored the man of fire and thunderstorms needed to have another encounter with God. But first he is told to eat and rest. Commentators have often made much of how physically tired Elijah must have been when you read of his activities leading up to this time. They are right but it's what is happening inside Elijah that has exhausted him.

Have you noticed how athletes react after a long gruelling race? The winner wants to do a lap of honour. He is bursting with life while those behind come in and grind to a halt and fall into someone's arms or sit on the ground. I can almost guarantee if they had come in first they would be bouncing around the track. Take another analogy of two armies who have been fighting on the battlefield for months. Their leaders know that what determines the outcome of the conflict isn't just the weapons and the training, but the soldiers' morale. A demoralized army, church or Christian who is beaten on the inside will soon experience defeat on the outside.

Elijah had stood up to Jezebel for years and hadn't run before. He was a man who wasn't pushed around by devilish threats. He could not be defeated on the outside unless something had happened to him on the inside. He had heard Jezebel's threats, now he needed to hear God's voice and God showed him seven thousand others in Israel that had not bowed the knee to false gods. Ahab may be king and Jezebel queen but Jehovah sovereignly reigns and rules and He will deal with them. Elijah has to come to a place where his hope is rooted in God alone, not in revival or miracles or even in pulling down demonic strongholds.

Discouragement is so destructive because it is the loss of courage and hope. When this happens our faith and confidence are undermined because *"faith is being sure of what we hope for and certain of what we do not see"* (Hebrews 11:1). Therefore our hope must always be focused on and rooted in God. This is one of the great recurring themes of Scripture. If this is not the case the enemy is manoeuvring us for disappointment and despair. God is sovereign – He knows what He is doing. So let me give a warning, "Those whose hope is in what they expect God to do more than in who He is, will get discouraged and confused when things don't happen the way they expect. The devil knows if he can destroy hope he can destroy faith. Therefore our hope must always be first and foremost established in who God is."

I pray and believe for revival, but there is a danger that we can get so caught up with what we expect and want God to do that we become discouraged when things don't happen the way we anticipate. The same thing is true with healing. I believe absolutely that God heals today. I have seen Him do it and love to pray for people who need His healing power. But my faith and my hope must be in a Sovereign loving God; otherwise I will be confused and distraught when things don't happen the way I expect. He is always Jehovah before He is *Jireh* (provider) or *Rophi* (healer).

> *"Be strong and take heart,*
>   *all you who hope in the* LORD.*"*   (Psalm 31:24)

> *"[B]ut those who hope in the* LORD
>   *will renew their strength.*
> *They will soar on wings like eagles;*
>   *they will run and not grow weary,*
>   *they will walk and not be faint."*   (Isaiah 40:31)

William Carey

William Carey is the founder of modern missions. In the eighteenth century he traveled to India with his wife and children, a five-month long, weary journey. He faced constant trials and hardship with finances, health, climate and disease. When they landed they were unsure whether the East India Trading Company, that controlled the area they were to settle in, would send them all back as the company did not want missionaries educating the natives. They had to take shelter in the Danish settlement at Seerampore where God graciously gave them favor with the Danish governor.

It was seven long years before Carey baptised his first convert. Many had shown interest but when it came to the final step of renouncing the caste system that controlled India they backed away. With great joy he held his first baptismal service. There were just two candidates, one was an Indian convert, Krishna, and the other was Carey's own son, Felix. Yet a very dark cloud rested on this joyous event. Six years before, just after arriving in India, his youngest child Peter aged just five died of fever and dysentery. As he baptised his first convert it was in the knowledge that his fellow missionary and dear friend Dr Thomas had been taken ill and was suffering from temporary insanity. It was necessary to have him restrained in the mission house. In another room in the same house his beloved wife Dorothy was suffering the same malady of mind and also had to be restrained. They later recovered but the trials and problems never went away.

Four years earlier Carey had written in his journal:

"There are grave difficulties on every hand, and more are looming ahead, therefore we must go forward."

He wrote to the Baptist Missions Society in England:

"I think it is very important to send more missionaries hither. We may die soon, and if we have no successors in the work, it will be a lamentable circumstance, and very much retard the spread of the Gospel. It is very important that we have a succession to hold forth the Word of life."[7]

Carey labored in India for more than forty years, never once returning to his native England. In March 1812, a devastating fire swept through the missionaries' printing plant and warehouse. They lost a large amount of newly cast type, nearly all of their Indian versions of the Bible, the Bengali Dictionary, and much vital equipment. Twenty years of non-stop labor were gone within a few hours. How would he respond to this crushing devastation? Undismayed, he declared:

"God will certainly bring good out of this evil and promote our interests. He will never forsake the work of His own hands."[8]

He wrote to his pastor-friend, Andrew Murray, in England:

"The ground must be laboured over again, but we are not discouraged. We have all been supported under the affliction, and preserved from discouragement. To me the consideration of the divine sovereignty and wisdom has been very supporting. I endeavored to improve this our affliction last Lord's day, from Psalm 46:10, *'Be still and know that I am God.'* I principally dwelt upon two ideas: God has a sovereign right to dispose of us as He pleases and we ought to acquiesce in all that God does with us and to us."[9]

Within months they began to understand why the "disaster" had occurred. When news of the fire reached England many people were awakened from their spiritual lethargy. Thousands became burdened for the lost and were moved to give sacrificially for the spread of the Gospel. Out of a seeming tragedy a new missionary zeal was born and the work in India advanced as never before.

The Apostle Paul was very honest about his own struggles with despair and discouragement He told the church at Corinth:

> *"We do not want you to be uninformed, brothers, about the hardships we suffered in the province of Asia. We were under great pressure, far beyond our ability to endure, so that we despaired even of life. Indeed, in our hearts we felt the sentence of death. But this happened that we might not rely on ourselves but on God, who raises the dead. He has delivered us from such a deadly peril, and he will deliver us. On him we have set our hope that he will continue to deliver us."* (2 Corinthians 1:8–10)

Paul's hope was in God and His eternal purposes. He went on to tell them:

> *"Therefore we do not lose heart. Though outwardly we are wasting away, yet inwardly we are being renewed day by day. For our light and momentary troubles are achieving for us an eternal glory that far outweighs them all. So we fix our eyes not on what is seen, but on what is unseen. For what is seen is temporary, but what is unseen is eternal."* (2 Corinthians 4:16–18)

In the last letter Paul wrote he knew his time may be short as he awaited his execution at the blade of a Roman axe, but his words to Timothy are full of faith and hope, *"I know whom I have believed, and am convinced that he is able to guard what I have entrusted to him for that day"*(2 Timothy 1:12). Years before when Paul found himself in jail for the first time in Philippi, God sent an earthquake, now in jail for the last time the devil is going to send an executioner. But Paul wasn't confused or despairing. He was persuaded of God's love and power and his hope for the future was in God's plan and purposes for him and not any edict that Caesar may give. His heart was set on God.

During the 1920s George Herbert Mallory led three expeditions to climb Mount Everest. The first expedition failed, as did the second. Then, with a team of the best quality and ability, Mallory made a third assault in 1924. But in spite of careful planning and extensive safety precautions, disaster struck. Mallory and climbing partner Andrew Irvine disappeared in heavy weather, never to return. (A 1999 expedition found Mallory's frozen body 27,000 feet up Everest's north face.) When the survivors returned to England, they held a banquet saluting those who were killed during Mallory's final expedition. As the leader of the survivors stood to acknowledge the applause, he looked around the hall at the framed pictures of Mallory and his comrades who had died. Then he turned his back to the crowds to face the huge picture of Mount Everest that stood looming like a silent, unconquerable giant behind the banquet table. With tears streaming down his face, he addressed the mountain on behalf of Mallory and his dead friends. "I speak to you, Mt. Everest, in the name of all brave men living and those yet unborn. Mt. Everest, you defeated us once; you defeated us twice; you defeated us three times. But, Mt. Everest, we shall someday defeat you, because you can't get any bigger and we can."[10]

Mallory's grandson, George Mallory II, reached the Everest summit in 1995.

Chapter 13

What Has Captured Your Heart?

Lord Jesus, do whatever you need to do in me
to accomplish all you desire to do with me and through me.

These seven tests will help to show you what has captured your heart. Don't rush through them but take your time and allow the Holy Spirit to speak to you.

One

What do you think about when not thinking about anything in particular? Where do your mind and emotions go? What tunes are you whistling and songs are you humming? What are your dreams and desires? How long does it take when you wake up in the morning for your thoughts and feelings to turn towards God?

What we think about and desire the most are the things that have captured our heart.

Two

When you are tempted to sin and are sure no one will find out, what has captured your heart will determine your response – the businessman overseas, those touring with the team, the money no one will miss, the lie nobody can discover. What governs your integrity and loyalty to those you love is what has captured your heart. D.L. Moody used to say, "Character is what you are in the dark." Reputation is what men think you are, character is what God knows you are.

Three

Jesus said what is stored in your heart will come out of your mouth. If you want to know what has captured a person's heart, listen to what they say and the way they say it. Dr Oswald Chambers used to say, "If a sinner wishes to understand his heart, then let him listen to his own mouth in an unguarded frame for five minutes."[1]

Four

Our priorities and the things we value most reveal what is in our heart. Jesus said, *"For where your treasure is, there your heart will be also"* (Matthew 6:21).

"The ancient city of Pompeii was buried under a thick layer of lava and ash by the sudden, violent eruption of Mount Versuvius in AD 79. During excavations a body was found that had been embalmed by the ashes of the volcano. It was that of a woman. Her feet were turned toward the city gate, but her face was turned backward toward something that lay just beyond her out-stretched hands. The prize for which those frozen fingers were reaching was a bag of pearls." What has captured our hearts becomes such a part of us that even though grabbing for a bag of pearls is absurd when you are about to be burned to death, you just can't help yourself.

Another equally absurd thing was taking place when they were manning the barricades in Moscow 1917 and preparing to fire the first shots that would launch a Communist revolution around the world, church dignitaries were holding a special meeting in the same city. It was called for the specific purpose of deciding what color robes should be worn at a certain ecclesiastical festival.[2]

A heart captured by God is not controlled by money, religion or anything else but by a desire to *"seek first the kingdom of God and His righteousness"* (Matthew 6:33, NKJV).

Five

What makes you laugh? There is a German proverb that says, "One shows his character by what he laughs at." If the devil can get you to laugh at sin it won't be long before you are committing it.

I'll never forget the testimony of a new Christian about what happened as she watched a certain programme on television with her husband. She had been a Christian for about a year but her husband wanted nothing to do with her new found faith.

One evening they were watching one of their favorite comedians, Dave Allen. She hadn't seen him for some time and was looking forward to the show. It wasn't too long into the programme that she felt uncomfortable about the content and manner of some of his jokes, and commented on how crude he was, adding, "He's changed since the last time I saw him." Her husband responded, "He hasn't changed, you have."

Six

How do you react when you don't have time to think about it? When someone bumps into you – upsets you and hurts you what's your reaction? What's inside comes out. It reveals so much about who we really are. The next time you get angry and upset and want to strike back, ask yourself, "Why did I react like I did?"

When Jesus went to his hometown of Nazareth He was given the honor of speaking in the synagogue, as He had become quite a famous preacher. He had already been ministering for almost a year as recorded by the first five chapters of John's Gospel. The people were intrigued and amazed at the stories they heard about Him. Before He had been fixing furniture, now He was mending broken bodies. He stood and read from the scroll of the prophet Isaiah, proclaiming that His mission and ministry was to bring healing and to set captives free because the anointing of the Spirit of God was upon Him.

So far so good, and the congregation loved it. Then Jesus said something that exposed their religious pride and nationalistic prejudice. *"Surely you will quote this proverb to me: 'Physician, heal yourself! Do here in your hometown what we have heard that you did in Capernaum'"* (Luke 4:23). They were hanging on His every word expecting an awesome demonstration of power but instead He revealed what was within them:

> *" 'I tell you the truth,' he continued, 'no prophet is accepted in his hometown. I assure you that there were many widows in Israel in Elijah's time, when the sky was shut for three and a half years and there was a severe famine throughout the land. Yet Elijah was not sent to any of them, but to a widow in Zarephath in the region of Sidon. And there were many in Israel with leprosy in the time of Elisha the prophet, yet not one of them was cleansed – only Naaman the Syrian.' "*   (Luke 4:24–27)

When they heard this they were filled with rage and wanted to kill Him. What caused such a murderous spirit when only moments before they all spoke well of Him? He had offended their minds to reveal and bring forth what was really in their hearts.

There was another occasion when Jesus did such a thing but the response was completely different. A Canaanite woman came to Him asking for mercy because her daughter was suffering terribly from demonic possession. Jesus answered that He was sent only to the lost sheep of Israel, and it was not right to take the children's bread and toss it to their dogs. He was offending her mind but it brought forth one of the most moving and powerful responses recorded in the Gospels:

> " 'Yes, Lord,' she said, 'but even the dogs eat the crumbs that fall from their masters' table.' Then Jesus answered, 'Woman, you have great faith! Your request is granted.' And her daughter was healed from that very hour."   (Matthew 15:27–28)

Seven

Billy Graham tells the story, that when the Standard Oil Company (now Esso) were looking to open up their operations in the Far East, they found a man they thought perfect to represent them. John Mott had been a missionary there for many years. They offered him $20,000 to work for them, a staggering amount at that time. He turned them down. They increased their offer to $30,000 and again he said no. They came back with $40,000 and once more he turned them down. They asked him what was wrong with the offer, didn't he think it was big enough? He told them, "There is nothing wrong with the amount but your job is too small, God has called me to be a missionary."

You can tell what has captured your heart by the extent to which "you cannot be bought".

There was an elderly gentleman sitting in a café talking with an attractive young lady. In the course of the conversation he pointed to a well-dressed young man seated at a corner table. "See that fellow over there, if he offered you a million pounds to sleep with him would you do it?" She thought briefly and said, "For a million pounds yes I would." A few moments later he pointed to another man standing at the opposite end of the room, "See him over there, if he was to offer you £10 to sleep with him would you?" Her reply was indignant, "Of course not, what kind of person do you think I am?" He replied softly, "I've already found that out, I was just trying to establish your price."

After moving into our present house we discovered it had been used a few years previously as the setting for a television soap opera. I realised the property was probably still on some sort of TV register and wondered what to do if they ever asked to use the house again? As I prayed about it, God reminded me it wasn't "my house" it was His. My wife and I were only stewards of it. I was then sure that He wouldn't want His house to be used as a place where scenes were shot that would portray sin as a form of entertainment. I prayed, "Jesus, even if they offered several hundred pounds a day the answer would be no." Immediately the thought came, "But what if they offered several thousand pounds a day or even fifty thousand pounds a week?" I felt God say, "If I say no it's no whether they offer five pounds or five million, the amount is immaterial to Me and to the extent you love Me with all your heart the amount will have no power over you."

Chapter 14

A Heart After God

When God wants to measure a man
He puts the tape around his heart and not his head.
(Scottish Proverb)

One Sunday morning at a well-to-do uptown church, an old man came in wearing worn out boots, grubby overalls and a ragged shirt. Some of the members got very upset and sent a note to the minister asking him to do something about it. So at the end of the service he greeted the newcomer and pointedly suggested that he pray about how God would have him dress next Sunday if he came back to that church. However, the following week he showed up looking no better. So the pastor took the man aside again and asked him what God had told him concerning how he should dress for their church. The old man smiled as he replied, "Well, believe it or not, I did speak to the Lord, but He didn't know how to dress for this particular church either because He's never been here Himself."

When the prodigal son came home to his father he too was not looking or smelling too good. A stint with the pigs had seen to that. But his father rejoiced at what had obviously happened within him and threw his arms around him smell and all. It's also true the prodigal didn't stay that way, the best clothes were ordered immediately but the way he came was the only way he could come. People change when we first accept them as they are.

Gift and character

The world is obsessed with image and reputation. God is concerned with integrity and character. *"Man looks at the outward appearance, but the* Lord *looks at the heart"* (1 Samuel 16:7). Samuel was told this when anointing a successor for King Saul,

118

who despite his own impressive outward stature had failed so miserably within. Saul was head and shoulders above other men but God was looking for a man of the heart. Character is about the heart, and it is this that determines the long haul. It is only a heart after God that can sustain the anointing and carry the gifting. God's gifts are irrevocable, they are grace gifts not given because we earn or deserve them. Even someone who backslides will continue to function in their grace giftings for a time. God's blessing doesn't always mean that we are living the way He wants. It has been said that the atheist's most embarrassing moment is when he feels profoundly thankful for something, but cannot think of anybody to thank. If God can bless an atheist He can bless anyone.

The person living in adultery makes the foolish assumption that he can get away with it and still minister effectively because people are saved and healed when they minister. Like Samson, who was powerfully anointed yet internally bankrupt, they say "while in the arms of Delilah", " 'I'll go out as before and shake myself free.' But he did not know that the LORD had left him" (Judges 16:20). There comes a day when the anointing has gone.

Samson still knew all the right moves and what to say but the anointing had finally lifted. Even though the gifts are without recall they need the anointing to function. The gifting without the anointing is like a rocket without fuel. It still looks the part but it's not going anywhere or taking anyone with it.

Mercifully there is a way back when this happens, but it's not easy and doesn't come cheap. It's the way of the cross, dying to self and yielding to God no matter what the consequences. For Samson it came during his time in a Philistine prison, blinded physically but beginning to see again spiritually. When a great leader of God falls, the world always demands its entertainment, and so Samson was called out to perform for him and his God to be humiliated before the Philistine mob and their god Dagon. Chained between the two pillars that supported the temple Samson prayed the first unselfish prayer we hear from his lips, "[Lord], *let me die with the Philistines!*" When exactly the moment came that he understood that his great strength didn't come from within himself or his own abilities we are not told, but now he knows it is only God who can give him back what he has lost.

The life of Saul is a story of tragedy, and tragically like him some are never restored. Anointed and empowered by God Saul managed to unite and establish the kingdom of Israel. He was a great warrior (Saul has slain thousands the people chanted) and had considerable giftings and prophesied when the Spirit of God came upon him. Yet he became insane. Tormented by his own insecurity and jealousy he began to rule by fear and madness and even consulted a witch.

His successor was to be a man who was more concerned with inner passion for God than outward power from Him, a man *"after God's own heart"*, because only such a person can truly represent God and be trusted with all God desires to do through him. While it is true that God loves all His children the same it is not true that He can trust them all the same. He is able to trust some far more than others because they have learned to trust Him and their hearts have been captured by Him.

After David was anointed as the future king, it was not long before he found himself facing a giant when Israel was battling the Philistines in the valley of Elah. Eliab his elder brother had been rejected by God when Samuel was told he was not the one to succeed Saul and his words to David are full of scorn and ridicule revealing his own heart, *"Why have you come down here? And with whom did you leave those few sheep in the desert? I know how conceited you are and how wicked your heart is; you came down only to watch the battle"* (1 Samuel 17:28). He accuses David of having a wicked and conceited heart after what God has said about him being a *"man after his own heart"*. The devil will always accuse and try to undermine what God seeks to establish in our lives. Eliab's words exposed the condition of his own heart and why God rejected him.

Apart from Jesus there is more said about David than any other individual in the whole Bible. There are sixty-nine chapters written about him in the Old Testament and fifty-nine references to him in the New Testament. I have often wondered what exactly God meant when He said David *"is a man after my own heart"*. It couldn't mean that David was sinless because no one is. The honesty of Scripture records David's failures not just his successes. David's heart was passionate for God and purified through his trials and suffering. He had a heart that loved to praise and worship even when others criticised him for it. He was more concerned about intimacy with God that authority from Him:

> *"My heart says of you, 'Seek his face!'*
> *Your face, LORD, I will seek."*   (Psalm 27:8)

Such a heart longs to worship and it is not bothered whether it's hymns or choruses, new or old, guitars or organs it simply wants to reach out and embrace God.

A heart after God is willing to wait for God's way and time to fulfill His promises. It was more than twenty long years before David was anointed king over the whole nation. It's only a relationship with God that can sustain you through such times. God must always be more important than the promise or the blessing. Such a heart is more in love with the giver than the gift.

We read in Psalm 78:72 that David led Israel with integrity of heart. In mathematics an integer is the opposite of a fraction. An integer is a whole complete number with no division while a fraction is a divided and fragmented whole. David prayed,

> *"Teach me your way, O LORD,*
> *and I will walk in your truth;*
> *give me an undivided heart,*
> *that I may fear your name."*   (Psalm 86:11)

He did not have a sinless heart but he did have a single heart after God.

But what happens when such a person sins? One night as David walked in the palace garden he saw one of the most dangerous sights known to man – a UFO – "an unclothed female object". He lusted after her, took her for himself and arranged the death of her husband Uriah. For almost a year David lives with the deceit and the sin. We know of no psalms or songs he wrote during this time. He still carried out the governing of the nation but this must have been his darkest hour. When the prophet Nathan confronted him with his sin, his response is not to have him silenced or added to his list of crimes and executed, but he exclaimed, *"I have sinned against the LORD"* (2 Samuel 12:13). Public sin requires public repentance and David's repentance was so public that over 3,000 years later we read about it in Psalm 51. Note what he says as he cries out to God to be restored:

> *"Create in me a pure heart, O God,*
> *and renew a steadfast spirit within me."*   (Psalm 51:10)

Sin is a heart issue and so is repentance.

A heart after God isn't only about where you are but also the direction you are going in. Imagine a straight line numbered from 1 to 10. The place of being born again is 1 and 10 is to be totally perfected. On this line at number 6 is one of the church's "leading lights". He has been saved a long time. At number 3 is a recent convert who still has major issues and problems he is working through. Amazingly it is this person God is mightily using while the one at number 6 is feeling a little resentful of the new upstart in the fellowship. Why is God so powerfully using one and not the other? The recent convert may only be at number 3 but was at number 1 only a few months before and he has a passionate heart after God. While the old timer at number 6 was at number 8 a few years ago and has become cold, formal and critical. What determines our effectiveness in the kingdom of God isn't only where we are at, but is the direction in which we are going. God would rather use a private who has a passion to fight than a general who only wants to retire.

The prayers of a captured heart

Robert Murray M'Cheyne was one of Scotland's greatest preachers. He ministered at the Church of Saint Peter in Dundee and during 1839 saw a great revival throughout the city and that part of the nation. One of his most famous prayers was, "Lord make me as holy as a redeemed sinner can be." The sincerity and reality of his praying were evidenced by the fact that people would be moved to tears just by seeing him in the pulpit or walking down the corridor of the church.[1]

He was a very learned man who knew Hebrew well and wrote his diary in Latin. He was conversant with the Greek classics, was a gifted musician and wrote hymns. He was also a fine painter but he is remembered most of all as a man of prayer. Churches larger than his offered a rich purse for his ministry but he graciously refused them all. He was contented with his lot because no church could offer him more time for prayer.

There is a story told of a visitor to his church in Dundee, after he had died. The sexton showed the visitor around. Some of M'Cheyne's books were still there. "Sit down here," said the sexton leading the young visitor to the chair M'Cheyne used to sit and pray in. "Now put your elbows on the table." The visitor obeyed. "Now put your face in your hands." The young man obeyed again. "Now let the tears flow. This was the way Mr M'Chyene used to pray." Then the amazed visitor was led into the very pulpit where the impassioned M'Cheyne had once poured out his soul to God and God's message to the people.

"Put your elbows on the pulpit," instructed the old sexton. "Put your face in your hands." The young man obeyed. "Now let the tears flow. That was the way Mr M'Cheyne used to do it."[2]

Before revival fires spread across Wales in 1904 God was preparing His people. One such man was the Welsh evangelist Seth Joshua. Dr Peter Joshua tells the story of how the fire and passion of God was burning in his father's soul in the days preceding the revival. He tells how he had been missing school and had gone to the Sophia Gardens in Cardiff, near where he lived, to catch some tadpoles in a jam jar. He spotted his father walking in the park and ran and hid behind some bushes.

> "As he came near I was frightened as I heard that he was crying (something I thought my dad would never do), and as he went by he was saying, 'Please God, give me Wales. Please God, give me Wales,' and kept saying this as long as I could hear him. After a while I ran back home, and while I had to explain to mother I had missed school, I asked her what was wrong with Dad, and told her that I had heard him crying and saying, 'Give me Wales.' She ruffled my hair and said, 'You'll understand one day.' God never did give Wales to my Dad, although He gave him many souls, but one day he was preaching and when he made an appeal Evan Roberts was the only one who stood to his feet and trusted the Saviour. God never gave Wales to my dad, but He gave Wales to Evan Roberts."[3]

One of the most moving prayers I have ever read was of a young man who not many years later was to give his life in seeking to reach a remote tribe deep in Ecuador's rain forest with the Gospel. Years before, while a student at Wheaton College he was meditating on the words, *"He makes his ministers a flame of fire"* (Hebrews 1:7, KJV), and he wrote in his journal a prayer of a man with a captured heart:

> "Am I ignitable? God deliver me from the dread asbestos of other things. Saturate me with the oil of Thy Spirit that I may be aflame. But flame is transient, often short lived. Canst thou bear this my soul, short life? In me dwells the Spirit of the great short lived, whose zeal for His Father's house consumed Him. He has promised baptism with the Holy Spirit and with fire. Make me Thy fuel O flame of God."

Jim Elliot died in January 1956 along with four other young missionaries speared to death by the stone-age killers of the Auca Indians. He was just twenty-eight years old and the world called it a tragedy, but it lit fires of missionary zeal that blazed around the world. A few years later, Jim's wife Elizabeth returned to the place of his death and brought the love of Jesus to those who had murdered her husband and saw them turn to the Lord.

The prayers of a captured heart are powerful and passionate. In Psalm 27 David declares:

> *"The Lord is my light and my salvation –*
> *whom shall I fear?*
> *The Lord is the stronghold of my life –*
> *of whom shall I be afraid? . . .*
> *Though an army besiege me,*
> *my heart will not fear."*   (Psalm 27:1, 3)

Even though Jerusalem was the nation's capital and called David's stronghold because of its natural and military fortifications, David knew that it was the Lord, and the Lord alone, who was the stronghold of his life.

He goes on to tell us his greatest desire:

> *"One thing I ask of the Lord,*
> *this is what I seek:*
> *that I may dwell in the house of the Lord*
> *all the days of my life,*
> *to gaze upon the beauty of the Lord*
> *and to seek him in his temple.*
> *For in the day of trouble*
> *he will keep me safe in his dwelling."*   (Psalm 27:4–5)

David's heart was captured by God and such a heart cannot be taken captive and defeated by fear or by all the physical and spiritual armies in this world. Such a heart made David a powerful warrior and even more a passionate worshiper.

A heart after God is a captured heart that calls you into His presence. Where is your heart calling you?

> **"My heart says of you, 'Seek his face!'**
> **Your face, Lord, I will seek."**
>   (Psalm 27:8, my emphasis)

"The widest thing in the universe is not space,
it is the potential of the human heart.
Being made in the image of God,
it is capable of almost unlimited extension
in all directions.
And one of the world's greatest tragedies
is that we allow our hearts to shrink
until there is room in them
for little beside ourselves."
(A.W. Tozer)

Notes

Introduction

1. William Barclay, *The Gospel of Matthew* (Edinburgh: Saint Andrew Press, 1975), p. 253.

Chapter 1: The Primary Target

1. Ravi Zacharias, "The Lostness of Humankind", *Preaching Today*, Tape No. 118.
2. John Wimber, *Power Evangelism* (Hodder & Stoughton, 1985), p. 74.
3. William Barclay, *The Gospel of Luke* (Edinburgh: Saint Andrew Press, 1975), p. 136.
4. Charles Colson, *A Dangerous Grace* (Thomas Nelson, 1994), p. 47.
5. Richard Wurmbrand, *In the Face of Surrender* (Bridge Logos, 1998), p. 209.
6. Alexander Solzhenitsyn, *The National Review*, 22 July, 1983.
7. *Life and Letters of Charles Darwin*, Vol. 1 (New York: D. Appleton & Co., 1911), p. 29.
8. Dr Victor Pearce, *Evidence for Truth, Science* (Eastbourne, Sussex: Evidence Programmes, 1993), p. 121.
9. Adrian Desmond and James Moore, *Darwin* (London: Michael Joseph Ltd, 1991), p. 476.
10. Ibid, p. 477.
11. English psychiatrist Dr Rankine Good links Darwin's health symptoms with his feelings of resentment towards his tyrannical father and says, "Thus, if Darwin did not slay his father in the flesh, then he certainly slew the Heavenly Father in the realm of natural history." Cited from Ralph Colp, *To Be an Invalid* (University of Chicago Press, 1977), p. 77.
12. Dr Victor Pearce, *Evidence for Truth, Science* (Eastbourne, Sussex: Evidence Programmes, 1993), p. 122.
13. Ibid, p. 123.
14. Ibid.
15. Joel Achenbach, "Life beyond earth", *National Geographic*, January 2000, p. 45.

Chapter 2: Money, Pride and Sex

1. Brian H. Edwards, *A People Saturated with God* (Evangelical Press, 1990), p. 65.
2. Tina Sinatra with Jeff Coplon, *My Father's Daughter* (Simon and Schuster UK, October 2000).
3. *Leadership* magazine, Spring 1990, pp. 118–119.
4. *A Minister's Obstacles* (Baker Book House, 1964), p. 41.

Chapter 3: Sex

1. William Barclay, *The Letters to the Galatians and Ephesians* (Edinburgh: Saint Andrew Press, 1975), p. 100.
2. *Daily Mail*, 22 November, 1999, article by Richard Pendlebury.
3. *Leadership* magazine, 2000.

Chapter 4: Idols in the Heart

1. *Foxe's Book of Martyrs* (Fleming H. Revell, 1968), p. 13.
2. William Barclay, *The Gospel of Matthew* (Edinburgh: Saint Andrew Press, 1975), p. 115.
3. Johann Sebastian Bach, quoted in *The Teaching Home*, December 1992.

Chapter 5: The Dangers of a Divided Heart

1. I decided not to name the person I am referring even though he is mentioned in the *Charisma* magazine interview with his wife. The man is seeking to rebuild his life and ministry and I pray for his complete restoration. The only reason I share the story is because it describes what can happen to anyone and illustrates how a person powerfully anointed falls into sin.

Chapter 6: Healing the Wounded Heart

1. Jim Carrey, cited from *Third Way* magazine, January, 2002; submitted by Richard Frank, Upminster, Essex, United Kingdom.
2. William Barclay, *The Letter to the Hebrews* Edinburgh: Saint Andrew Press, 1975), p. 125.
3. Ibid.
4. Philip Yancey, *Where is God when it Hurts?* (Marshall Pickering, 1977), p. 134.
5. Kenneth S. Wuest, *Great Truths to Live By* (Eerdmans, 1952), p. 115.
6. Martyn Lloyd-Jones, *The Puritans, Their Origins and Successors* (Banner of Truth, 1987), p. 355.
7. Ibid, p. 349.
8. *The Works of Jonathan Edwards*, Vol. 1 (Banner of Truth, 1974), p. 104.
9. Ibid, p. 207.
10. Ibid, p. 127.

Chapter 7: Keep Your Heart Soft

1. Vance Havner, *Leadership* magazine, Summer 1994. Quoted in "Moody", March 1993.
2. Jim Graham, *The Giant Awakes* (Marshalls, 1982), p. 65.
3. C.H. Spurgeon, *The Treasury of David* (Baker Book House, 1981), p. 52.
4. James S. Hewitt, *Illustrations Unlimited*.

Chapter 8: Forgive

1. Stanley W. Green, *The Canadian Mennonite* (9-4-00), p. 11.
2. Paul Easterbrooks, *Secrets to Spiritual Success* (Sovereign World, 1996), p. 59.
3. Philip Yancey, *What's So Amazing About Grace?* (HarperCollins, 1997), p. 99.
4. Selwyn Hughes, *Every Day with Jesus – One Year Devotional* (CWR), p. 155.
5. Corrie ten Boom, *Tramp for the Lord* (Hodder and Stoughton, 1974), pp. 55–57.
6. Martyn Lloyd-Jones, *Spiritual Depression, Its Causes and Cures* (Pickering and Inglis, 1965), p. 67.
7. Ibid, p. 68.

Chapter 9: Righteousness

1. Melvin Banks, *Faith Unlimited* (Marshall Pickering, 1991), p. 25.
2. Peter Graystone, *Ready Salted*.
3. Kurt E. Koch, *Occult Bondage and Deliverance* (Kregel Publications, 1970), p. 16.
4. Roland Barton, *Here I Stand*, biography of Martin Luther (Lion, 1978), p. 65.
5. C.H. Spurgeon, *Lectures to My Students* (Baker Book House, 1977), pp. 1–2.

Chapter 10: Thankfulness

1. Richard Wurmbrand, *Sermons in Solitary Confinement* (Hodder and Stoughton, 1969), p. 77.
2. *The Journal of John Wesley* (Send The Light Productions), p. 419.
3. James S. Hewett, *Illustrations Unlimited* (Wheaton: Tyndale House, 1988), p. 264.

4. Derek Prince, *Thanksgiving Praise and Worship* (Word Books, 1991), p. 11.
5. Selwyn Hughes, *Every Day With Jesus Yearly Devotional* (CWR), p. 156.

Chapter 11: The Word

1. Brian H. Edwards, *Revival – A People Saturated with God* (Evangelical Press, 1990), p. 64.
2. Ernest Gordon, *Miracle on the Kwai* (Collins Books, 1963), p. 88.

Chapter 12: Don't Lose Heart

1. James Ryle, *The Hippo in the Garden* (Highland Books, 1992), p. 98.
2. John Pollock, *Wilberforce* (Lion, 1977), p. 82.
3. Ibid, p. 105.
4. Ibid. p. 308.
5. Kevin A. Miller, Vice-President, *Christianity Today International*; source: CNN.
6. Deauville, *William Carey*.
7. *God's Hall of Fame* (Barbour Books), pp. 8–22.
8. Bill Mills and Craig Parro, *Finishing Well in Life and Ministry* (Leadership Resources International), pp. 101–102.
9. *God's Hall of Fame* (Barbour Books), pp. 8–22.
10. James S. Hewett, *Illustrations Unlimited* (Wheaton: Tyndale House, 1988), p. 131.

Chapter 13: What Has Captured Your Heart?

1. Selwyn Hughes, *Every Day with Jesus – One Year Devotional* (CWR), p. 160.
2. William Gowland, *Militant and Triumphant* (London: Epworth, 1957), p. 26.

Chapter 14: A Heart After God

1. Brian H. Edwards, *Revival – A People Saturated with God* (Evangelical Press, 1990), p. 53.
2. Leonard Ravenhill, *Revival Praying*, pp. 59–60.
3. Brynmor P. Jones, *Voices from the Welsh Revival* (Evangelical Press of Wales).